# LIFE ON EARTH
# THE FIRST HUMANS

## THE DIAGRAM GROUP

Facts On File, Inc.

**Life On Earth: The First Humans**

Written, edited, and produced by Diagram Visual Information Ltd

| | |
|---|---|
| *Editorial director:* | Denis Kennedy |
| *Editors:* | Bender Richardson White, Gordon Lee |
| *Contributors:* | Quartz Editions, John Stidworthy |
| *Indexer:* | Martin Hargreaves |
| *Art director:* | Roger Kohn |
| *Senior designer:* | Lee Lawrence |
| *Designers:* | Anthony Atherton, Christian Owens |
| *Illustrators:* | Pavel Kostal, Kathleen McDougall, Coral Mula, Graham Rosewarne |
| *Picture researcher:* | Neil McKenna |

Facts On File, Inc.
132 West 31st Street
New York NY 10001

For Library of Congress Cataloging-in-Publication Data, please contact Facts On File, Inc.
ISBN 0-8160-5050-3

Facts On File books are available at special discounts when purchased in bulk quantities for businesses, associations, institutions, or sales promotions. Please call our Special Sales Department in New York at 212/967-8800 or 800/322-8755.

You can find Facts On File on the World Wide Web at: http://www.factsonfile.com

Printed in the United States of America

EB Diagram   10   9   8   7   6   5   4   3   2   1

This book is printed on acid-free paper.

# Contents

# Introduction

THIS BOOK is a concise, illustrated guide to what we know about the evolution of our own human species from its early ancestors. Texts, explanatory diagrams, illustrations, captions, and feature boxes combine to help readers grasp important information. A glossary clarifies the more difficult terms for younger students, while a list of websites provides links to other relevant sources of additional information.

Chapter 1, *Who Are We?*, places us in the context of the natural world and our relatives among the animals. It also looks at some of the earliest fossils that are thought to have some connection with human ancestry, up to and including the australopithecines.

Chapter 2, *Becoming Human*, tells the fossil history of humans, from the first primitive toolmakers living in Africa, up to the appearance of our own species, *Homo sapiens*, that is now entrenched worldwide.

Chapter 3, *Keeping Track of Change*, looks at some of the main changes that have taken place in the human body during its evolution, and takes a brief look at modern methods of tracing ancestry and what they tell us about our past.

Chapter 4, *Life Long Ago*, looks at many aspects of human life, including speech, hunting, farming, and art, and details some of the things that are known about ways of life in the distant past.

Chapter 5, *Great Ages*, looks at the changing conditions of life, both environmental and technological, that humans have lived through, in some of the great "Ages" that have been named by paleontologists and archeologists.

Chapter 6, *Around the World*, takes a continent-by-continent approach to human history, focusing on stories that illuminate the past.

Chapter 7, *On the Track*, looks at the business of finding fossils, giving an account of just some of the famous human fossil finders. Examples are also given of some notable finds, and some major disappointments, including a hoax.

Chapter 8, *Talking Points*, provides a little more detail on the process of understanding fossil remains, and also takes a look at what the future may hold in store for the human species.

*The First Humans* is one of six titles in the Life On Earth series that looks at the evolution and diversity of our planet, its features, and living things, both past and present.

The series features all life-forms, from bacteria and algae to trees and mammals. It also highlights the infinite variety of adaptations and strategies for survival among living things, and describes different habitats, how they evolved, and the communities of creatures that inhabit them. Individual chapters discuss the characteristics of specific taxonomic groups of living things, or types of landscape or planetary features.

Life On Earth has been written by natural history experts and is generously illustrated with line drawings, labeled diagrams, and maps. The series provides students with a solid, necessary foundation for their future studies in science.

*Like horses, dogs, camels, whales, and mice, human beings are mammals: warm-blooded, backboned animals that are nourished when young on milk from the mother's body. What makes us different from other creatures in both appearance and behavior?*

HUMANS ARE SOCIAL ANIMALS. We live in groups and take on specific roles within society. But a social way of living is not unique and is found in many simpler creatures such as ants. These tiny insects organize themselves into large groups. A single nest has a queen and many workers, and sometimes specialized soldiers. They operate with the minutest of brains. Yet they work together to construct a home for themselves. In some species, a number will join forces to build bridges of their own bodies over which others may cross. In a similar fashion, bees cooperate to find new sources of nectar and to make honey.

Most of the behavior of these animals is instinctive. That is, it is built in to the animal and does not need to be learned. Instinct can produce some amazing results. For example, when the weather gets chilly, monarch butterflies automatically set off from Canada and fly thousands of miles (km) to Mexico for a warmer environment. Then, in time for the North American summer, a new generation manages to find the route back again.

A distinctive human feature is our great capacity to think and reason, and to learn from experience. We have very large brains compared to the size of our bodies, and the ability to use language. We are the most adaptable creatures ever to have lived. As well as our reasoning ability, we

**Ancestor?**

*Remains of animals, such as* Proconsul *from about 18 million years ago, suggest the appearance of our distant ancestor. It was monkeylike, and walked on all fours; an analysis of its teeth helps to place it on the ape and human branch of the tree of life.*

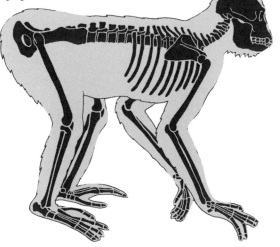

**Bones from Kenya (right)**

*A stamp marks the discovery of* Proconsul *bones on an island in Lake Victoria, Kenya, East Africa.*

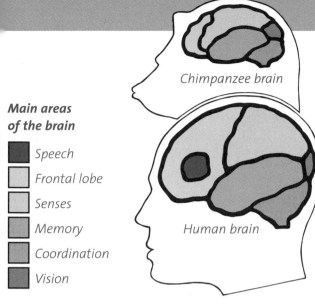

*Chimpanzee brain*

**Main areas of the brain**

- ■ Speech
- □ Frontal lobe
- ▨ Senses
- ▨ Memory
- ▨ Coordination
- ▨ Vision

*Human brain*

**DID YOU KNOW?**
The meaning of the Latin name of our species, Homo sapiens, is "wise man." It is a clear reference to our greater brain capacity and general intelligence compared to other animals. These include the early hominids from which paleoanthropologists (scientists who study our prehistoric ancestors) believe we evolved.

have many feelings: emotional responses to certain situations; an esthetic appreciation (an interest in distinguishing, or analyzing, the beautiful, or beauty); and both a visual and a verbal sense of humor.

In most other respects, there are not too many differences between us and those animals that are our closest relations. Scientists have discovered that we are, in fact, very close to chimpanzees in our genetic makeup. Almost 99 percent of our genetic material is exactly the same. Of course, apart from our brains, we are set apart from chimpanzees by some physical features. We do not have a full coating of body hair; we perspire more profusely, walk habitually on our hind legs, and, perhaps most important of all, can use our hands to manipulate our surroundings.

What we do not know, however, is whether today's human beings have reached the pinnacle of our species' evolutionary advancement, or whether we will continue to evolve.

*Comparing size*
Proconsul major *was bigger than a present-day chimpanzee.* Proconsul heseloni *was smaller, the size of a baboon.*

*On the basis of some fossilized, broken pieces of jaw, and just a few teeth unearthed in 1932 and dated to between 12 and 14 million years ago, scientists thought they had found the earliest of our ancestors. Were they right?*

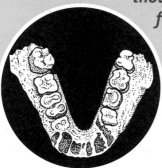

**A human relative?**

*The shape and size of Ramapithecus' teeth led to the idea that it might have been related to humans, but the jaw shape suggests otherwise.*

**W**HAT EXCITEMENT there was when these fragments of jaw were first discovered! Scientists concluded they had belonged to a creature weighing no more than 40 pounds (18 kg). What persuaded some paleoanthropologists that it could be a hominid were its teeth, which were about the same size and shape as those of present-day humans.

It appeared to have lived in open country, and there was a suggestion that it was bipedal. Other experts, however, disputed these findings. It was impossible, they said, to conclude from its teeth that this species had walked upright without seeing its leg bones.

The American scientist Dr G.E. Lewis was the first to study the remains, and he declared it to be a human ancestor. However, the debate continued until finally, in 1976, a complete jawbone was unearthed. At this point, the majority of scientists began to support the view that the teeth and jawbone did not come from a hominid after all, but were in fact from an ape.

Ramapithecus and the larger, similar Sivapithecus are now thought to be on another side of the ape family tree, not especially closely related to the branch that gave rise to humans. Modern orangutans, not humans, are thought to be descended from Sivapithecus. The current consensus of opinion is that the fossil species walked on all fours most of the time, rather than being bipedal (i.e., two-footed).

This group of apes produced a huge species, Gigantopithecus, which can be thought of as a giant, ground-living, orangutan. It lived from 10 million years ago to less than 1 million years ago. It has even been suggested that the occasional reported sightings of the manlike "yeti" in remote parts of the Himalayas could be explained if a few of these ancient animals have somehow managed to survive to this day. Up to the present time, however, no-one has produced a live specimen.

**IT'S A FACT!**
The names given to both Ramapithecus and Sivapithecus have an Indian origin, reflecting the area of their first discovery. Ramapithecus was called after the Hindu god Rama, and Sivapithecus after another deity, Siva. *Pithecus* means "ape."

*In 2001, remains between 5.2 and 5.8 million years old were unearthed in Ethiopia, Africa. They were claimed to be the earliest hominids. Then a French team found even older bones, dating as far back as 6 million years. They dubbed them "Millennium Man" because they had been excavated at the start of this new era.*

THE SO-CALLED "MILLENNIUM MAN" was given the scientific name, *Orrorin tugensis* because the word *orrorin* means "original man" in a language local to the Baringo region in Kenya where the remains were found. Some skeptical scientists say it is too chimplike to be classed as a hominid. They doubt it was capable of walking upright. However, the femur (upper leg bone) has a ball joint angled in at the top, and some people consider that bipedal walking may have been possible.

Ardipithecus ramidus (5.2–5.8 million years old) is known from fragments. A toe bone suggests to some scientists that an upright stance was possible. The jaw had small canines, and the other teeth show some similarities to humans.

For Sahelanthropus tchadensis, discovered in Chad in Central Africa, we have an almost complete skull 6 million years or more old. It has been nicknamed "Toumai." Is it an early hominid or an ape?

The study of fossils of possible human ancestors is full of bones of contention. Scientists are sure that humans and apes had a common ancestor—perhaps 8 million years ago. However, it is not easy to ascertain the exact line of ancestry that led to modern humans. This is not surprising. Fossil remains are rare, and are often just fragments. Teeth are the hardest parts of the body, and are most likely to survive, but isolated teeth tell us

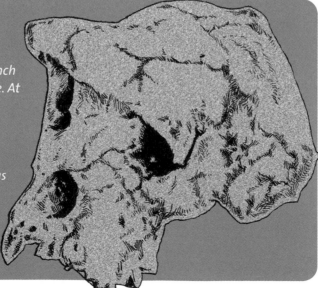

*A human relative?*
*"Toumai" may be the oldest known fossil from the human branch of the ape family tree. At the time it lived, a number of species of apelike creatures roamed much of Africa. The Sahara was then green, rather than a dry desert.*

little. Most other fossils are pieces of jaw or bone fragments. A whole skull or leg bone, let alone a whole skeleton, is a rarity. It has been said that all the known fossil bones of early man would not be enough to fill the graveyard of a small country church. Year by year, new fossils are excavated and add to our knowledge, but there is still much to find out.

Paleoanthropologists are keen to add to the sum of human knowledge by promoting their own findings. It is sometimes claimed that the results of a find "will completely change our view of human evolution." Sometimes this is so, but a new find usually adds only a tiny piece to the jigsaw puzzle of anthropological knowledge. Too often, it is difficult to see where the new piece fits. This is why there is continuous disagreement between scientists about the significance of new finds.

## IT'S A FACT
Paleoanthropologists work in many ways. They study the geology and history of a region. They read books and papers by others in their profession to keep abreast of new theories. Sometimes they obtain clues about where to excavate through satellite and aerial images. But luck also plays a part, and many amazing discoveries are made entirely by chance.

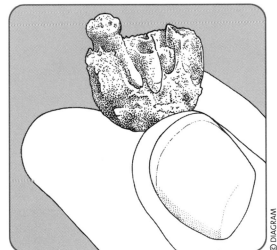

**A human ancestor? (above)**
Ardipithecus *remains are usually fragments, such as part of a jaw with teeth. They suggest that this species had some similarities with later ones on the human side of the family tree.*

© DIAGRAM

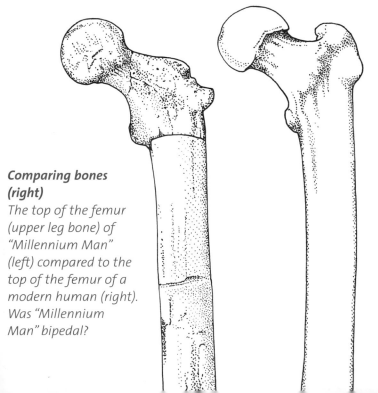

**Comparing bones (right)**
*The top of the femur (upper leg bone) of "Millennium Man" (left) compared to the top of the femur of a modern human (right). Was "Millennium Man" bipedal?*

**The skeleton of one of the oldest hominids discovered to date was named Lucy because the song** Lucy in the Sky with Diamonds **happened to be playing when the remains were brought back to the campsite. What would she have been like?**

LUCY WAS HER NICKNAME, but scientists named the species itself Australopithecus afarensis, after Afar, the region of Ethiopia, where the remains were discovered. Lucy's fossilized remains show that she was small in stature, just 4 feet (1.3 m) tall, and that she had short legs, long arms, and a slightly hunched posture. Her hands and feet also suggest that she might have spent time swinging in the trees when not walking upright. Tracks found of others of her species, meanwhile, indicate an arched foot, a structure found only in humans. Most of her skull was missing, but from other specimens that have been found, the brain size was only about 26 cubic inches (430 cm³), no bigger than a chimpanzee's. Lucy lived about three million years ago.

Australopithecines like Lucy were just one of several species of Australopithecus that lived in Africa between 4 and 1 million years ago.

*Lucy's skeleton (left)*
*About 40 percent of Lucy's skeleton was found.*

**Australopithecus boisei** *(right)*
*Mary Leakey found this skull in Africa.*

**Australopithecus vs. modern human (right)**
*This skull has a low forehead and flat face. Brain capacity is less than half that of modern humans.*

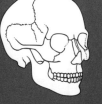

Australopithecus afarensis *skull*

Modern human skull

Australopithecus africanus was only 3–4.5 feet (1–1.38 m) tall, lightly built, and could walk upright. Although its teeth were larger than ours, they show some similarities. The brain was a little larger, compared to body size, than that of a modern ape. Australopithecus africanus is known from South and East Africa.

Some of the later australopithecines were larger and more robust. Australopithecus robustus was about 4 feet 3 inches (1.32 m) tall. The cheek teeth were large, and many show signs of heavy wear, suggesting a diet of tough plant foods. The biggest australopithecine known was Australopithecus boisei. Some individuals may have been 4 feet 5 inches (1.37 m) tall. Found in East Africa, this species had enormous jaws and cheek teeth, leading to the nickname "Nutcracker man." However, calculations of the force that the jaws could exert show that its bite was no stronger than ours, and it may have fed mostly on fairly soft leaves.

**Australopithecus**
*Apelike, but walking on two legs, an early type of* Australopithecus *was probably ancestral to later human types.*

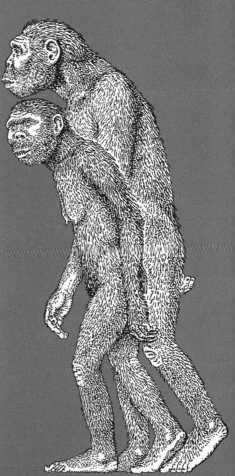

**DID YOU KNOW?**
Australopithecus means "southern ape," so Australopithecus africanus means "African southern ape" and Australopithecus robustus means "stocky southern ape." Australopithecus boisei is named after a London businessman who offered funds to the dig where its remains were found.

# The first tool-users

*When scientists set about piecing together literally hundreds of skull fragments found at an African site in 1972, it was like trying to solve the most complicated jigsaw puzzle ever devised.*

IT TOOK paleoanthropologist Maeve Leakey and her colleagues a full 6 weeks to reconstruct the remains of a skull unearthed by her husband Richard's team. The final result provided valuable clues to the capabilities and way of life of the hominid species Homo habilis, first discovered 11 years earlier at Olduvai Gorge, Tanzania.

This species lived alongside the australopithecines more than two million years ago, but there were distinct differences. Its brain cavity size, for example, was considerably larger—more than 40 cubic inches (655 cm³) which suggests much greater intelligence. Most scientists now agree Homo habilis was one of the first hominid species to use tools to butcher animals for food. When the opportunity arose, members of this species probably scavenged, taking what meat remained on

*Is this the face of our ancestor?*

*An attempt to put flesh on the skull provides a glimpse of what* Homo habilis *may have looked like about two million years ago.*

## IDENTIKIT

A particular feature put Homo habilis apart from the apes— the fact that this early ancestor of ours put its weight across the whole sole of the foot when walking erect. Apes put their weight on the outside of their soles. Homo habilis was far from being a modern human. Nevertheless, its finger bones look as though they would have been able to grip objects well, and it was able to make simple tools from pebbles. It probably also made simple wooden tools, but these would have rotted. Its scientific name means "handy man."

the carcasses of any dead creatures that they happened to find when going about their daily lives. Fossilized teeth of Homo habilis suggest that this hominid was an omnivore and ate many different sorts of vegetation as well as flesh.

Homo habilis is the earliest species placed in the genus Homo, to which we belong. The species, or something very similar, later gave rise to humans. We now know that mankind originated on the continent of Africa, and that human origins lie further back than previously believed.

**DID YOU KNOW?**
The toolkit of *Homo habilis* consisted of pebbles and small rocks from which flakes were knocked off by hitting with another rock or piece of wood. A pebble might be struck just on one side, or on opposite sides. This left it with a sharp edge. Either the pebble, or the flakes, could be used for cutting meat, or as weapons. These tools were made two million years ago and had almost completely disappeared by 1.5 million years ago. They may have been simple, but they were also obviously very useful.

**Homo habilis**
*This species was less than 5 feet (1.5 m) tall, and lightly built.*

© DIAGRAM

*About 1.9 million years ago, a new type of hominid evolved in Africa. It eventually moved into Asia and Europe. This new hominid was recognizably human, but it differed from modern-day people in many respects.*

THE HOMINID known as *Homo erectus* ("upright man") was similar to us from the neck downward. It stood upright, but the bones were more robust than ours and their muscles bigger. This species would have been used to physical exertion. However, the braincase was low and there were prominent brow ridges in the skull. The brain capacity was about 61 cubic inches (1,000 cm$^3$), roughly three-quarters of that of a modern human.

The best fossil we have of this type of human, in fact the most complete early human fossil known, was found near Lake Turkana in Africa. It includes the skull and much of the skeleton. It is of a boy about 13 years old, who was already 5 feet 4 inches (1.6 m) tall. If the growth pattern of *Homo erectus* was similar to ours, he might have been 6 feet (1.8 m) tall if he had lived to be an adult.

**Celebration**
*A 1982 Kenyan stamp issued to mark the origins of mankind.*

**Turkana boy**
*The oldest-known human skeleton belongs to a young* Homo erectus *from Kenya.*

**Homo erectus (left)**
*He was possibly the first hominid to discover how to make and use fire.*

All the oldest fossils of *Homo erectus* have been found in Africa but, by one million years ago, some of these people had reached Southeast Asia. Fossil-hunters first found this species in Asia, Java, and China many years before the earlier fossils were found in Africa. *Homo erectus* also reached Europe. This type of human eventually died out perhaps fewer than 50,000 years ago.

A particular type of stone tool, the "Acheulean hand axe," is associated with creatures that evolved from *Homo erectus*. First discovered in the northern French village that gives them their name, these tools have since been found in many places in Europe. Shaped like a teardrop, many of these hand axes are beautifully fashioned, and come in a range of sizes, presumably depending on the user. They were used less as axes than as the stone-age equivalent of a handy penknife. They could be used for cutting, butchery, or digging. They were so useful that they were common until about 200,000 years ago.

**Holding a hand axe (above)**
*It is probable that the user grabbed the axe by its rounded butt, and then exerted downward pressure to cut meat or dig up edible roots.*

© DIAGRAM

*As well as making tools to a thought-out pattern, it has been suggested by some scientists in the past that Homo erectus made practical use of fire in parts of China, Europe, and Africa.*

IN THE COOLER northern regions of the world, *Homo erectus* used caves for shelter, as it did in China, where the remains of the local *erectus,* "Peking Man," were found. Evidence reveals that they made shelters of interlocking branches held in place with stones. Some of these primitive huts could have held 20 individuals.

It appears that from birth to adult, the brain of *Homo erectus* may have grown three-fold, much more than the doubling seen in apes. This suggests a long childhood, much more comparable to ours than the swift maturity of apes. Other behavior also seems to have been more advanced than what went before.

By about 300,000 years ago, many humans were beginning to show a mixture of characteristics that are found in *Homo erectus,* and those that are seen in modern people. It is difficult to tell whether these people were changing and evolving where they lived, or if the old inhabitants were being replaced by new waves of settlers with more "modern" bodies, or if the old established people

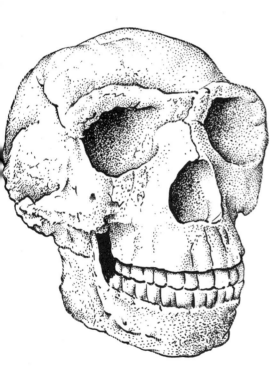

**Skull of Peking man (above)**
This example of Homo erectus *had a smaller skull than modern humans.*

**Early European finds (right)**
*This map shows the main sites where early human remains have been found.*

were interbreeding with newcomers. There is some evidence that most new trends in human development have originated in Africa. The new species then moved out to the wider world, gradually replacing those who were there before.

"Heidelberg man" lived in Germany and other parts of Europe 500,000 years ago. He is known from just a lower jaw that was massive but chinless. His teeth, though, were very similar to ours. The Swanscombe skull, discovered in Britain, is a partial skull from 250,000 years ago, with a braincase that held a modern-sized brain. Some African skulls from 200,000 years ago still had heavy bones with brow ridges, but with a modern brain size. People were becoming more like us, but were still much more solidly built.

An ice age, with a series of glaciations, started about 1.7 million years ago, and this had a major impact on human life, as well as plants and animals, in northern areas of Europe and Asia.

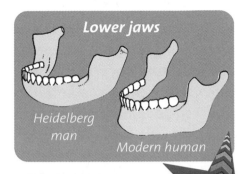

*Lower jaws*

Heidelberg man

Modern human

**WAY BACK IN TIME**
From the remains of post holes and stone supports, we know that Heidelberg man camped near the sea at what is now Nice, in France, some 400,000 years ago.

**A flimsy shelter**
*Oval huts made from interlocking branches housed hunters visiting the shores of the Mediterranean Sea.*

© DIAGRAM

*In 1856, as a limestone quarry was being blasted in the Neander Valley near the town of Düsseldorf in Germany, miners suddenly noticed a few odd-looking, bowed, leg bones, and part of a skull, within the rubble. Little did they realize the great age and importance of the remains they had stumbled upon!*

NEANDERTHALS were named after the German valley where their remains were first found. Neanderthals are thought to have evolved from people like Heidelberg man about 200,000 years ago. They lived in Europe and the Middle East until about 35,000 years ago, and no one is certain why they disappeared after that. It is possible they interbred with modern humans, or were conquered or simply out-adapted by them.

The original Neanderthal fossil was bent as a result of bone disease. Reconstructions based on this skeleton have led to Neanderthals being pictured as bent, stooping creatures of low intelligence. This was far from the truth. They were short, stocky, and muscular; their physical

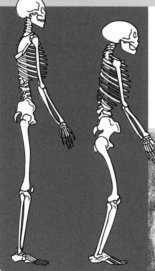

**Comparing bones (above)**
*A Neanderthal skeleton (right) compared to a modern human (left).*

**Early finds (right)**
*Caves were probably vital shelters for Neanderthal people in the bitterly cold Ice Age winters.*

stature was rather like that of present-day Inuits, which is not surprising as the Neanderthals lived in an ice age, and needed to conserve heat. Most Neanderthal remains have been found in caves where they sheltered from the cold. Such sites, yielding the remains of more than 200 Neanderthals in all, have been found in places as far apart as Spain, Gibraltar, France, Italy, Germany, Croatia, the Czech Republic, Russia, Uzbekistan, Israel, Iraq, and Morocco.

The special stone tools that the Neanderthals developed are known as Mousterian tools after the site at Le Moustier, France, where they were first found, and comprise scrapers, tiny saws, borers, sharpeners, and knives. The range of implements lent themselves to slaughtering, cutting, and skinning animals. Neanderthals were obviously intelligent people, with the skills to survive in a bitter climate. In spite of their brow ridges and sloping foreheads, these people, on average, had brains slightly larger than those of modern humans.

It has been suggested that Neanderthals were the first people to bury their dead in a ritual fashion, with food provided for the deceased to enjoy in an afterlife. They may also have been naturally compassionate. The remains of a very old man crippled by arthritis, and half-blind long before he died, suggest that he was looked after while in a frail condition.

**DID YOU KNOW?**
As the result of finding, in Germany, a single sticky fingerprint on some fossilized wood, scientists suggest that Neanderthals had the skill to burn birch wood slowly over fire to make a sticky tar, which they could use as glue in the manufacture of tools.

**Neanderthals**
*Female Neanderthals were slightly smaller than males, but also stocky.*

© DIAGRAM

*The chance finding of the ancient skeletal remains of a woman, three men, and a baby in a cave in western France back in the 19th century was to prove a landmark discovery. They were evidence of a new type of human. They are called the Cro-Magnons, after the place where they were first unearthed.*

**THE "OLD MAN OF CRO-MAGNON"** was given this nickname because, from his skull, scientists estimated he must have been about 50 when he died—a ripe old age for anyone living 35,000 years ago. How they came to perish together, no one knows. The woman's remains show she must have suffered an injury at some time.

Typical Cro-Magnons lived in Europe. In most essentials they were modern people who, by 40,000 years ago, were leaving remains in many parts of the world. Compared to Neanderthals, modern people have shorter faces, higher braincases, and high foreheads without brow ridges. A pronounced bony chin is also typical of modern humans. The jaw is smaller and the teeth more crowded. The brain size, at 85 cubic inches (1,400 cm³) was a little less than that of Neanderthals. Some Cro-Magnon men may have grown to 6 feet (1.8 m) in

*Burying their dead*
*Cro-Magnon burials, like these from Russia 23,000 years ago, show ornaments buried with what may have been high-ranking people. The old man (below) had been buried in fur clothes with over 1,000 beads and ornaments. The boys (right) had beaded furs, ivory bracelets, and spears made from mammoth tusks buried with them.*

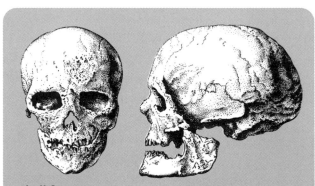

*Skull features*
*The Cro-Magnon skull had a flat face, a high forehead without brow ridges, and a protruding bony chin.*

**Cro-Magnon art**
The sudden flourishing of cave art and carving in Europe coincides with the arrival of Cro-Magnon people.

height and probably looked very much like today's human beings.

Most scientists think that modern humans originated in Africa and spread outward. But others think that various groups of humans grew more "modern" in different parts of the world from the more archaic human types. In some places, there is some evidence of Neanderthals and Cro-Magnons existing together, but by 30,000 years ago Neanderthals had more or less disappeared. Did the Cro-Magnons wipe them out? Did they just do better in competition for food and living places? Or did the two types interbreed? In many modern populations, a few individuals have rather sloping foreheads and brow ridges. Are these Neanderthal genes showing themselves?

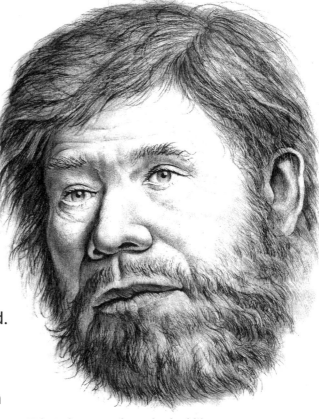

**What they may have looked like**
This artist's impression attempts to recreate the facial characteristics of a typical Cro-Magnon man.

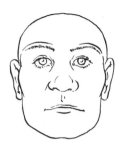

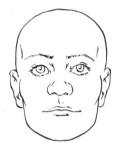

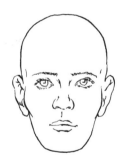

*About 40,000 years ago,* Homo sapiens *suddenly seems to have advanced by leaps and bounds, producing far more sophisticated tools and weapons, as well as outstanding works of art. Our species became far more creative, developed whole systems of social interaction, began to trade, and developed greater linguistic skills.*

IT IS PRESUMABLY the quick-wittedness and adaptability of *Homo sapiens* that has allowed our species to thrive. We took over the planet from other human types that had gone before. The Neanderthals faded out. The last ones lived in southern Europe, in what are now Croatia, Spain, and Portugal. Intriguingly, Joao Zilhao of Portugal's National Institute of Archeology discovered a juvenile skeleton in 1999, which appears to come from the very end

**Evolving heads (above)**
*These three heads suggest that the adult human face has tended to adopt a more juvenile appearance as it has evolved. The top face is Neanderthal (large jaw and nose, low cranium); the middle face is Cro-Magnon (smaller jaw and nose, higher cranium); and the bottom face is based upon an average human face of today (even smaller jaw and nose, still higher cranium).*

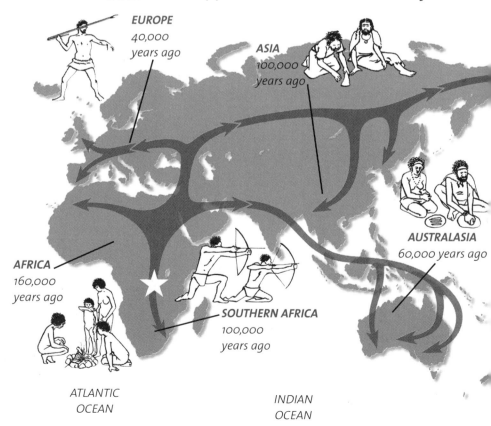

EUROPE
40,000 years ago

ASIA
100,000 years ago

AUSTRALASIA
60,000 years ago

AFRICA
160,000 years ago

SOUTHERN AFRICA
100,000 years ago

ATLANTIC OCEAN

INDIAN OCEAN

**Spread of modern humans (below)**
*What are generally accepted to be modern types of humans probably arose in Africa. Leaving Africa, they spread first to southern Asia and Australasia, then western Europe, and finally to North and South America.*

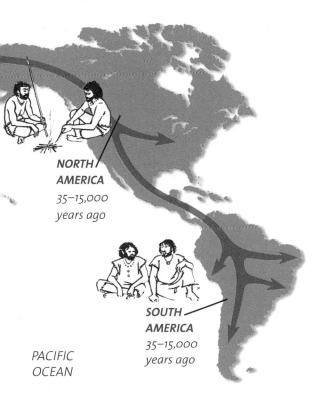

NORTH
AMERICA
*35–15,000
years ago*

SOUTH
AMERICA
*35–15,000
years ago*

PACIFIC
OCEAN

of the Neanderthal period. He interprets the skeleton as a Neanderthal-human hybrid. Other scientists believe, after looking at genetic evidence, that Neanderthals were too different for interbreeding to be common, and that modern humans simply displaced Neanderthals.

It was probably in the development of social behavior that modern humans excelled compared to Neanderthals. Modern human groups may have been larger, and their language better developed. The practice of burying the dead with various kinds of "treasure" suggests that groups were more complex and organized, with leaders who merited special treatment in life and death. The modern people were physically weaker than Neanderthals, but were on average taller.

The exact figures are disputed, and subject to change as more facts are established over the years, but we can discern the outlines of the spread of modern humans. Thoroughly modern types probably arose 160,000 years ago in Africa. By about 100,000 years ago they had begun to leave Africa. By 60,000 years ago, they had reached southern Asia and Australia. By 40,000 years ago, they had reached western Europe; by 35–15,000 years ago, they had moved into North and South America.

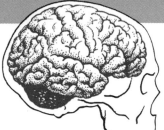

**Homo sapiens**
*Present day*
*Brain size: 85 cubic inches (1,400 cm³)*

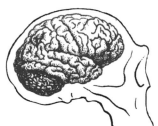

**Homo erectus**
*1 million years ago*
*Brain size: 61 cubic inches (1,000 cm³)*

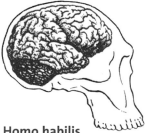

**Homo habilis**
*2 million years ago*
*Brain size: 40 cubic inches (655 cm³)*

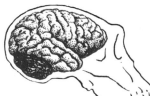

**Australopithecus afarensis**
*3 million years ago*
*Brain size: 26 cubic inches (425 cm³)*

*Australopithecines' brains were not much larger than those of the apes. In our ancestral line brains have greatly enlarged in just a few million years. In particular, the proportion and overall size of certain parts (lobes) of the brain, changed. The enlarged lobes have provided a greater capacity for memory and reasoning.*

SCIENTISTS have one great disadvantage when studying the evolutionary development of the human brain. Soft tissue tends not to fossilize, but rots, and so very little remains of ancient brain tissue. However scientists can measure the size of the cranium (braincase) and skull, and rely on clues left on the inner surfaces.

From the skulls of australopithecines we can tell that the frontal lobe, responsible for controlling movement and the emotions, was proportionately much smaller than it is in modern

**Erectus *vs.* sapiens**
Homo erectus *had strong jaw muscles, and the neck muscles were well developed to hold up the heavy face. In* **Homo sapiens** *the brain is bigger, the face shorter, and the head is more easily balanced on the vertebral column, requiring less powerful neck muscles. Muscles are reduced for the smaller jaws.*

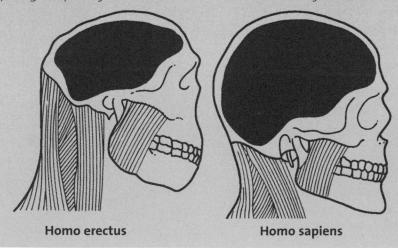

**Homo erectus**                    **Homo sapiens**

humans. However, the rear occipital lobe, which handles vision, was as well developed as ours.

The parietal lobe, with the role of taking in information, is about double the size it is in today's humans; and the temporal lobe, responsible for memory, more than three times the size. Australopithecines may have evolved to walk some of the time on two legs but their intelligence was limited, and perhaps little greater than that of their ancestors, the apes.

*Homo habilis*, however, had a greatly increased cranial capacity—about 50 percent more than the australopithecines; and *Homo erectus,* a further 50 percent more. But *our* brains are three to four times the size of those of our earliest forebears.

**DID YOU KNOW?**
The larger the brain, the more energy it requires in terms of an increase in calorie-rich foods. Our earliest ancestors were largely vegetarians and survived on a fairly meager diet. However, the gradual introduction of a wider range of foods, such as meat, boosted their calorie intake, and also helped to enhance their brainpower.

FRONT

Parietal lobe

Frontal lobe

Temporal lobe

Occipital lobe

Cerebellum

**The human brain**
*The brain is a complex structure in which different parts have contrasting functions. The outer layer, the cortex, controls movements and registers sensations. It contains vast numbers of brain cells. There can be 10,000 miles (16,000 km) of connecting fibers for these in 1 cubic inch (16 cm³).*

© DIAGRAM

*The skeletal remains of early australopithecines, show that they measured no more than 4 feet (1.3 m), and weighed about 65 pounds (30 kg). Modern adult men, on average, measure in the region of 5 feet 10 inches (1.78 m), and weigh about 150 pounds (68 kg). However, although we are taller than our ancestors, we are also far less sturdy.*

HUMANS HAVE SPECIALIZED in walking on hind legs. The top section of the legs slopes inward, and the knees are directly below the body. The legs swing backward and forward in the most efficient way. The backbone has an extra curve to help us to stand upright. The head, with its large brain, balances on top of the backbone. The changes that make us human have all occurred in the last few million years.

Another change in the human line is our precision grip. Most monkeys and apes have opposable thumbs and can hold branches and other objects. But humans have the best developed opposable thumbs. We pick up and manipulate varied objects, and perform precise movements with our hands. This ability, together with our large brain, has led to much distinctively human behavior.

**Evolution (right)**
*This illustration creates a sequence of development from* Australopithecus *to modern man, who is shown behind early* Homo sapiens *for comparison of size. Some changes shown are backed by fossils, while others are guesswork.*

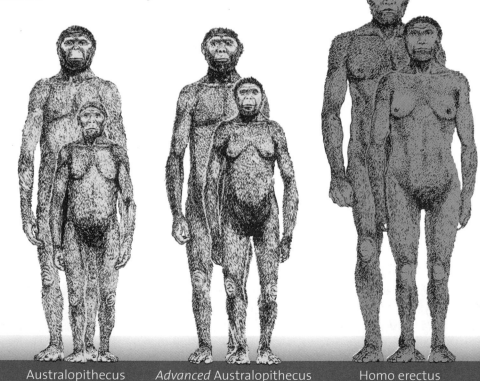

| Australopithecus | *Advanced* Australopithecus | Homo erectus |
|---|---|---|
| **2–3 million years ago** | | **1.5 million years ago** |

All these changes can be traced through hard parts preserved as fossils. Some changes leave no traces. For example, we assume that early australopithecines, like their ape cousins, were dark skinned. This seems reasonable, given their tropical origins, although some chimpanzees have light skin. For humans, light skins may be a recent phenomenon, developed when some human groups moved from the tropics to less sunny climates. We assume that australopithecines were furry, like apes. Modern humans are not. We have many hairs, but most so small and fine that we appear to be naked. We have many well-developed sweat glands, unlike apes. We do not know when the change took place as it does not show in fossils. The guess is that it took place when our ancestors began to undertake long periods of physical activity, for example running after prey during a hunt in the open. But nobody knows for sure how hairy *Homo erectus* was. Clothes have been used in cool climates for many thousands of years. Their wearers probably had skins like ours.

**IT'S A FACT**
Some changes are still in progress. Large jaws and teeth in our earliest ancestors gave way to the smaller teeth and jaws we have today. Even in the last thousand years, Europeans' jaws have changed slightly. Since we have eaten softer cooked foodstuff, the importance of large teeth has declined. Those people today with the largest teeth are usually from groups used to eating tougher foods raw.

*Early* Homo sapiens    *Modern man*

*1 million years ago*

**Walking upright (right)**
*Why did our ancestors first walk upright? To be able to see over tall savanna grasses, or to wade through shallow water?*

© DIAGRAM

# Another way to study ancestry

*One of the greatest discoveries of the 20th century occurred during the 1950s when two scientists revealed to the world that they had managed to break the genetic code. Francis Crick and James Watson, an Englishman and an American, were working at Cambridge University, England. For many years after their discovery, progress was slow but, by the end of the 20th century, enormous strides have been made in uncovering the genetic makeup of many organisms. This has given scientists another tool to use to test how closely different species are related.*

A MINUSCULE ARCHIVE of inherited information, known as DNA, is carried in the nucleus of every cell of every living animal and plant. Crick and Watson worked out that DNA was a long molecule with two strands that intertwine in a spiral known as a "double helix," and that the two strands fitted together with links of just a few types. The links provide a code that controls cell functions and characteristics, and through these determine the whole shape and function of the complete organism. Along the DNA are many code groups that make up "genes." These control your characteristics—whether you have brown or blue eyes, for instance, fair or dark hair, or a large or small nose. Half the genes in your cell nuclei come from your mother, half from your father.

Scientists guessed that animals that are most alike, and share a common ancestor, would have DNA and genes that are most similar. This seems to be the case. For example, your DNA is more like that of a cow than that of a worm or starfish. Usually the relationships suggested by the results of these comparisons confirm what was thought from the study of anatomy.

**DNA (left)**
*This is the name given to the inherited information carried in the nucleus of every cell of every living animal or plant.*

Scientists have discovered that the DNA of humans is very much like the DNA of chimps. In fact it is over 98 percent the same. This is the closest match for our DNA. The other apes are less like us in terms of genetic makeup.

These studies suggest that chimpanzees and humans had an ancestor in common not all that far back in time. The distribution of chimpanzees and the earliest hominid fossils make it fairly certain that this ancestor lived in Africa.

**IT'S A FACT**
Sometimes sudden leaps in evolution have occurred during the history of the world. Scientists explain this by pointing out that damage can occur to the genetic programming of cells so that imperfect replicas are inherited by the next generation. Differences will generally be so small that they are hardly seen, but it is possible for them to be far more marked so that physical features change very noticeably. This is true for both animals and plants.

*Behavior (right)*
*Jane Goodall made numerous studies of chimpanzees in the wild and found that their behavior was much more complex than had been previously realized.*

*Chimpanzee expressions (below)*
*Like us, chimpanzees communicate emotion by facial expressions. The chimps are shown in the following modes: **1** relaxed, **2** greeting, **3** smiling, and **4** angry.*

As well as the DNA in the nucleus, there is some in the mitochondria—tiny structures within the cell that act as its powerhouse.

MITOCHONDRIAL DNA plays no part in sex and reproduction, and is passed, unchanged, straight from mother to offspring. The only changes that take place are occasional random mistakes in its manufacture, known as mutations. In humans, a stretch of mitochondrial DNA has been sequenced, so that the chemical code along its length is known. Mutations are very rare here, but happen about once in 10,000 years. The generally stable molecule, with a known, expected mutation rate, gives an ideal tool for tracing human lineages through the mother's side.

Bryan Sykes, while Professor of Human Genetics at the University of Oxford, showed that DNA could survive in ancient fossilized bones. What is more, mitochondrial DNA showed that almost all the 650 million or more people of European origin, no matter where they may live in the world today, are descended from one of seven women. He dubbed them "The Seven Daughters of Eve."

Research on mitochondrial DNA has produced much of interest. Contemporary people of African descent are known to have more differences in their mitochondrial DNA, passed down through the female line only, than everyone else in the world put together. This suggests that modern humans first evolved in Africa, had longer there to evolve differences, and those that moved out were just a small section of the population.

Mitochondrial DNA also points toward Neanderthals being distinct from modern humans. Some scientists now believe all modern humans can trace our line back to one ancestral mother in Africa. She may have lived about 200,000 years ago.

*Structure of a cell (below)*
*The cell contains a nucleus with chromosomes that are made of DNA. Nuclear DNA comes half from the father, half from the mother. Mitochondria also contain DNA, but this is all from the mother.*

Mitochondrion - - -

Nucleus

Chromosomes

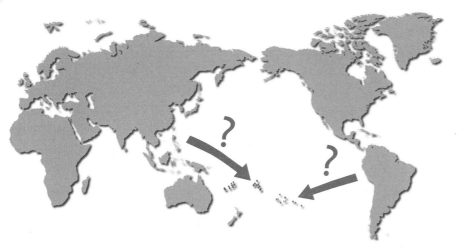

***Ancestors (left)***
*Was Polynesia populated by people from the Americas (as suggested by some sea currents), or from Southeast Asia (as suggested by their domestic animals)? The mitochondrial DNA of people in Polynesia actually proves to be like that of people in Southeast Asia.*

## DID YOU KNOW?

**1 2 3 4 5**

An invisible chain links your body to the earliest humans who inhabited the Earth. Genes (**1**) are the building blocks of your DNA (**2**). These genes are inherited from your ancestors. Each gene carries the instructions for the cells to form and perform their separate functions in your body. DNA (**2**) is assembled into chromosomes (**3**) which gather together (**4**) to form the nuclei of your cells (**5**). Each cell also carries certain non-nuclear genes transferred over a period of 200,000 years from the early modern humans to you.

© DIAGRAM

*Apes pick up and throw branches and stones as weapons. They also use twigs as tools to find food. However, when one of our ancestors shaped a piece of stone to make a better tool, he or she took the first step on the road to behavior that is characteristically human—the making and using of tools.*

THE FIRST TOOLS we know of, dating from almost three million years ago, are pebbles which had been struck to make an edge, and the sharp flakes that had been struck off them. But branches, animal bones, and antlers could well have been used as tools before then.

Following these simple tools, there was a long period during which *Homo erectus* made a rather limited, but no doubt effective, range of tools such as hand axes and cleavers. Early *Homo sapiens* probably started out with the same tool kit. From 100,000 to 35,000 years ago Neanderthals made more advanced tools. These included scrapers, backed knives, borers, and little saws, as well as points which were probably bound onto some kind of spear. Neanderthals used what is called a Levallois technique, striking a core stone of glassy material such as flint in such a way as to knock off a flake of a particular shape. The

**Making a flint tool (right)**
*The flint is roughly shaped with a stone hammer (top). A softer hammer of bone is used to refine the shape (middle). The edge is trimmed by "pressure flaking," which involves pressing a point on an edge until a small flake eventually splits off (bottom).*

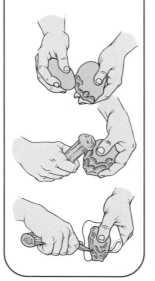

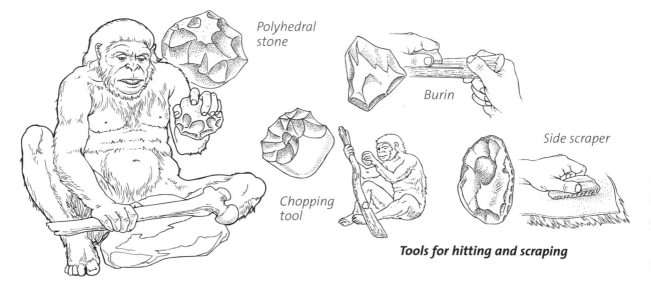

Polyhedral stone

Burin

Chopping tool

Side scraper

**Tools for hitting and scraping**

flakes were worked on further to make the finished article.

The Cro-Magnons who took over from the Neanderthals were even better at making tools. Several "cultures" of toolmaking are recognized, roughly succeeding one another in time in Western Europe. As time went by the workmanship became finer. Beautifully crafted, leaf-shaped blades, flint knives, arrowheads, and boring tools were made, and fine harpoons, fishing hooks, and spear points made of bone and ivory were in use. As the design of tools and weapons grew more sophisticated, hunting and fishing became more successful. This may have helped larger populations to survive.

In some parts of the world today, such "Stone Age" tools are still in daily use. Investigators have turned to groups, such as the bushmen of southern Africa, or Australian aborigines, to learn more about how the tools are made and used.

**DID YOU KNOW?**
At a site in Colorado, tools about 10,000 years old were discovered alongside hundreds of bison bones. This has led some experts to speculate that even this long ago there may been specialized butchers for the local community.

*a*  *b*  *c*

**Advanced tools**
*Late Stone Age people could use their sharp stone tools to make very fine, or complex, objects from bone and antler, such as harpoons **a** and **b**, or needles **c**.*

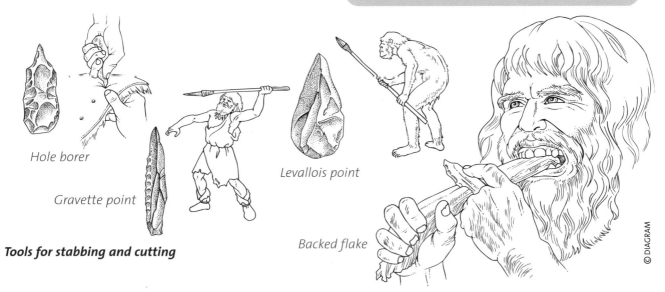

*Hole borer*

*Gravette point*

*Levallois point*

**Tools for stabbing and cutting**

*Backed flake*

© DIAGRAM

*Our earliest ancestors were probably not carnivores but gatherers, with a diet of nuts, plants, fruits, roots, eggs, and any other edible matter readily available. But we soon turned to scavenging for meat, and then to the kill, even before we had mastered the art of using fire for cooking.*

EVEN IF OUR ANCESTORS had very limited knowledge by today's standards, there is evidence they must have been wily. Recognizing how difficult it was to chase and catch animals on foot—the bow and arrow are a very recent invention—they regularly set traps for their prey. With luck, when large creatures were caught in this way, not only would there have been enough for many meals, but also skins and fur from which garments could be made. Whole tribes may have taken part in hunting excursions. Having been tracked down, a whole herd might be chased over cliffs, falling to their deaths below. The carcasses would then be retrieved, and the flesh removed from the bone with sharp cutting and scraping implements.

Other sneaky methods are known to have been used, too. Sometimes, for example, having disguised themselves in animal hides, hunters would creep up on prey, and then attack. Often it would be the youngest and weakest of a pack that would be chosen in this way. Small creatures may have been killed by stones—either thrown or used as a weapon in the hand—before a meal was made of them. When early humans went fishing, they probably simply used spears to stab at a larger catch. Later, specialized harpoons were used, and simple nets were used from the shore for trapping fish. Basket

**Hunted animals (below)**
*Our ancestors fed on a range of animals, from mammoths to tortoises, and also on fish and shellfish. Remains found at ancient campsites and caves often include the bones or shells of favorite foods. Marks of ancient tools often show how the flesh was cut off.*

*Cave painters (right)*
*Cave paintings often depict the animals that the people would have hunted. However, the most commonly painted animals do not always correspond to the most commonly found food remains.*

**DID YOU KNOW?**
A cache of 250,000-year-old elephant bones found in Spain—where this species once lived in the wild—seems to indicate that our distant ancestors regularly hunted elephants by driving them into pits or swamps. An animal this size provides plenty of meat. Horse meat was also a common food in prehistoric times, and is still eaten in parts of Europe today. A mass of horse remains dating back 17,000 years has been found in France. Herds were probably driven toward a cliff barrier before being slaughtered.

traps are another ancient method of catching fish. All these different methods of fishing are still used in some parts of the world today.

Were animals hunted exclusively for food? Large groups of skulls are sometimes found in caves. They may have been displayed as hunting trophies, but their precise arrangement also suggests that they may have been placed there for use in rituals or ceremonies. However, we still do not know their exact significance.

*Setting a trap (below)*
*Passing beasts, such as mammoths, often stumbled into thinly-disguised holes in the ground, and were then stabbed, or even clubbed, to death.*

© DIAGRAM

THE EARLIEST HOMINIDS that we know about—the australopithecines—were, like their relatives the apes, still mainly plant-eaters. The shape of their cheek teeth was good for chewing plants. The large and worn cheek teeth suggest that some of the big, robust australopithecines ate very tough plant stuff. Others ate mainly soft leaves, and *Australopithecus africanus* was probably a fruit eater, like a chimpanzee. This is confirmed by microscopic tooth wear. Different types of food make different patterns of scratches and tiny pits that can be seen on a tooth's surface by examination with a microscope. Scientists can distinguish between teeth that dealt with meat or plants. They may even be able to guess whether the plants were fruit, leaves, or tubers dug from the ground with grit attached.

*Although we are a long way from knowing exactly what our ancestors ate, we can still find clues. The shape and size of the jaws and teeth may suggest that they are geared to a particular kind of food. More information may come from the way the teeth are worn down. Sometimes there may be food remnants associated with the remains of early people or their campsites. What is certain is that food preferences have changed during our evolution.*

*Homo habilis* may have eaten some meat, but much of this may have been scavenged from other predators. Early on in human history, many of the animal bones that appear to have been cut or scraped with tools have animal tooth marks beneath the tool marks. With *Homo erectus*, meat seems to have increased in importance in the diet. Dangerous though it must have been, there are signs that these early people hunted animals ranging

**Throwing a spear**
*Cro-Magnons invented new techniques for hunting, including spear launchers to increase a throw's range and power, and hooks and harpoons to trap fish.*

from baboons to elephants. At some stage they also started to use fire, and this enabled them to cook and tenderize meat and the tougher vegetables. The ability to catch meat, a concentrated food, may have been one factor that allowed *Homo erectus* to move into cold lands.

Modern humans have mostly included meat in their diet. The proportion may have differed according to where they lived and what was available. In cold places, some tribes have lived largely off animal meat and fat. To our modern eyes, this may not seem the healthiest diet, but they probably needed all the calories that were available.

**IT'S A FACT**
Large brains are very expensive in terms of energy consumption. Weight for weight, brain tissue burns up far more energy than muscle. A human brain is about 2 percent of the body weight, but it uses 17 percent of the body's energy. Perhaps meat-eating was important in providing the energy for big brains. Then perhaps, larger brains led to more efficient tools and strategies for hunting.

**Hunting (above) and dismembering the carcass (right)**
*Although* Homo erectus *probably ate a lot of plant food, such as fruits and tubers, meat would have been prized as a very satisfying and nourishing food for the tribe.*

© DIAGRAM

Our ancestors must have needed to watch out for all kinds of predators, such as saber-toothed tigers, leopards, cave bears, and hyenas. But there is evidence both in Europe and North America that our forebears sometimes needed to watch out for members of their own species. Occasionally, at least, early humans resorted to cannibalism.

AT A CAVE SITE known as the Pit of Bones (in Spanish, *La Sima de los Huesos*), in a region called Atapuerca in northern Spain, paleoanthropologists have found the remains of some early humans. These fossilized bones include skulls, ribcages, and other body parts.

The most extraordinary thing about the finds, however, is that some of the bones, dated to about 800,000 years ago, show signs of having been scraped of flesh. They have marks of cutting, scraping, and hammering by stone tools, in exactly the same fashion as bones of food animals such as deer have been treated. We can only assume that this would have been done in order to cut off human meat to eat. Why such cannibalism took place is not clear. It could perhaps have been that the community was very short of

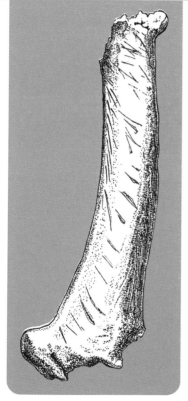

**Butchered human bone (above)**
A bone, with cut marks on it, produced by sharp stone tools.

food and turned to eating human flesh only as a last resort. Or is it possible some ritual was involved? Closer to the present-day, cannibalism has been rare, but in those groups that practiced it there was sometimes a belief that you could gain in strength or intelligence by eating someone with exceptional qualities. It may even have been that a family member was shown respect, after death, through his or her consumption.

Remains of Neanderthals found at Moula-Guercy cave in southeast France also show signs of flesh and bone marrow extraction. Two adults, two adolescents, and two children are thought to have been butchered 100,000 years ago. The braincases had been smashed, leading some scientists to suppose that the brains themselves may have been eaten, and one tongue had been removed.

**DID YOU KNOW?**
At a place called Cowboy Wash in southwestern Colorado, archeologists have found an ancient village site with the remains of seven unburied and dismembered bodies that show signs of having been prepared for meals. Examination of fossilized human excrement (known as coprolites) at the site also shows human remains in it. Some scientists think that the eating of the villagers' flesh, and subsequent defecation, may be a sign of the degradation of the local population by an invading tribe or group. But it is also possible that the human flesh may have been eaten during a dreadful famine. The climate is known to have gone through a period of terrible drought about then, before the village finally became uninhabited around CE 1150.

*Neanderthal cannibals (left)*
*There is no reason to think that cannibalism was a normal way of life for early humans, but it is known that, sometimes at least, people ate human flesh.*

©DIAGRAM

*The fossilized remains of our ancestors enable us to guess what they looked like and their way of life. Sometimes they can also tell of injuries sustained or diseases suffered during a lifetime. Wear and development of teeth may help to tell us how old an individual was when he or she died. The long bones, and their ends, also help in deducing age at death.*

LEG BONES of a female *Homo erectus* from about 1.6 million years ago found at Koobi Fora in East Africa tell of disease. They have a covering of disorganized bone cells, unlike the usual rigid pattern of strong bone. In modern times, such bone deformity is characteristic of too much Vitamin A. Hungry Arctic explorers who have fed on polar bear liver have died from Vitamin A overdose. Survivors may have bones damaged in the same way as the Koobi Fora woman. Perhaps she had eaten livers from large carnivores, such as lions.

Other *Homo erectus* bones, from Java, suggest that the individual suffered fluoride poisoning from a volcanic eruption.

Many Neanderthal specimens that have been discovered show pathological changes in the skeleton, probably reflecting the hard life that these people led. One famous Neanderthal specimen, the "Old Man of La Chapelle," found early in the 20th century, was almost complete. It was reconstructed at the time as a shambling, bent, apelike, subhuman. Fifty years later, the skeleton was looked at again by the English anatomist A.J.E. Cave with W.L. Straus, an American colleague. They found that this individual suffered from severe arthritis that had bent the spine. The average Neanderthal

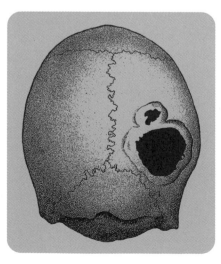

**Diseased bone (above)**
*This femur of a* Homo erectus *was found in Java.*

**Trepanning (left)**
*Perhaps the first of all surgical operations, this involved making holes in the skull (of a* Homo sapiens) *with sharp flint instruments possibly to release "spirits" to relieve an attack of madness, or an epileptic fit.*

was as upright as modern humans. In fact, Cave went as far as saying that had a Neanderthal been washed, shaved and dressed in a suit, he would not have stood out in a modern crowd.

In 1856, the first Neanderthal to be discovered also turns out to have had his share of problems. His left arm was broken, and would have been little use, and he was very arthritic. He must have survived as long as he did because of help from his community. In April 2002, a biologist working at the University of Zurich, Switzerland, reported on a skull he had studied. He found a hole probably caused by a blow from a tool wielded by another Neanderthal. But although Neanderthals were violent at times, small splinters of skull had clearly been reattached by someone who nursed the injured individual back to health. On this evidence, Neanderthals must have been socially aware and compassionate.

Some Neanderthal skeletal remains show evidence of rickets, a disease which bows the leg bones, and which is caused by dietary deficiencies. It is a condition that still occurs in impoverished communities today.

**Neanderthal bones**
*A discovery made at La Chapelle-aux-Saints revealed arthritic ends to long bones, and misshapen vertebrae, that belonged to an elderly Neanderthal man.*

© DIAGRAM

## PAST MATTERS

Injuries to Neanderthals may provide a real clue as to the type of life they led. Analysis of healed wounds on a large sample of skeletons shows that these occurred mainly to the area of the head and upper body. A similar distribution of injuries has been found in rodeo riders. It suggests that Neanderthals had close contact with large animals—not simply as riders, but rather as hunters at close quarters with the animals they had targeted for food.

*The continent of Africa is almost certainly the place of origin of our own species (Homo sapiens). Africa is joined to Asia and, via western Asia, to Europe. So it is not surprising that early people gradually spread into Europe and Asia wherever the climate and food supply would support them. However, Australia and the Americas are cut off from the "Old World" by major sea barriers. When and how did humans manage to reach them?*

SOME SCIENTISTS think that humans may have made the journey from Africa to Southeast Asia by wandering along the coasts, using the plentiful shellfish as a source of food. In spite of the distance involved, it might not have taken that long for the human range to expand. It has been calculated that if people moved east by just a mile each year, they would have traveled the whole way in fewer than 10,000 years. The process was probably much quicker.

At various times during the last ice age, when much of the world's water had been locked up in ice and glaciers, sea level has been much lower than now. Then, what are now islands in Southeast Asia—Java, and Sumatra, for example—were joined to the mainland. This allowed humans to colonize these areas. Australia remained an island, but could be reached on primitive boats that might not need to cross more than 40 miles (65 km) of sea at a time. Australia, with its warm climate, may have been peopled by modern man before cold

## IT'S A FACT

As our ancestors spread around the world, they encountered different climatic zones and their bodies adapted accordingly over many thousands of years. In hot climates dark or black skin was an advantage as it protected people from the Sun by the production of a pigment known as melanin. White skin does not readily produce this pigment and so peels and blisters in the very hot sunlight; it is more suited to cloudy, cooler regions, and absorbs just enough ultraviolet radiation to make adequate Vitamin D for a healthy body's needs. Those people with dark or black skin who live in more temperate parts of the world sometimes lack Vitamin D and develop rickets, a bone disease, as a result.

Ice Age Europe. Australia was certainly well populated by modern humans by 40,000 years ago. Some seem to have been there 60,000 years ago. From changes in animal life, and increases in bushfires that happened then, some scientists have speculated that humans might have been having an effect there more than 100,000 years ago.

It is not certain when the first people arrived in North America, but it was probably less than 20,000 years ago. By 11,000 years ago, people had spread throughout all of North and South America.

### Crossing the Bering Strait

*During the peaks of glaciation, there was a land bridge between Siberia and Alaska, now covered by the sea of the Bering Strait. This was a route that could be taken by humans, although conditions would have been very harsh at that time.*

© DIAGRAM

*Caves made good refuges for early humans to escape from the elements and wild beasts. Often rocky overhangs, rather than deep caves, provided shelter. Caves could also be used for storing food and as burial places. But not everyone lived where caves were available. What happened when early people ventured into open country?*

SHELTERS made in open country by early man have disappeared without trace in most cases, but a number of ancient homes have been found and excavated.

The first purpose-built homes took the form of tepees, tents, or huts, constructed around a basic framework of branches. Early in the year 2000 CE, signs of homes built 500,000 years ago by *Homo erectus* were discovered near Tokyo, Japan. These can be dated accurately because they are above a layer of volcanic ash from a recent eruption nearby. In the layer of ash there are ten holes that were dug for poles that supported the structures, five for each hut. Stone tools were also found. The framework may have been covered with leafy branches. It is not known if such a hut would be used for a long time, or just for a night or two. Later in 2000 CE, even older hut foundations were discovered in Japan, so we now know that *Homo erectus* was making these shelters at least 600,000 years ago.

In the Ukraine archeologists have found evidence of large huts made by Neanderthals. The hut would have been covered

***The first man-made dwellings (below)***
*This illustration shows a range of shelters, made for protection in open country, which were constructed 400,000–500,000 years ago.*

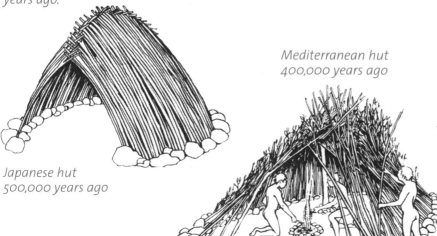

*Japanese hut
500,000 years ago*

*Mediterranean hut
400,000 years ago*

*Russian hut
40,000 years ago*

with animal skins. Mammoth bones weighed down the edges. Neanderthals were evidently good tent builders. At a cave near Nice in the south of France, Neanderthals even built a tent inside a cave entrance to provide greater protection from the cold air.

Later, modern types of human also hunted in the cold Ukrainian climate and made houses out of skins with mammoth bone supports. Some such homes, known as longhouses, could be over 100 feet (33 m) long and 18 feet (5 m) across. Three or more oval-shaped huts were linked by a single roof covering so that several families could winter under the one roof. Smaller huts were probably built for summer use.

*Ukrainian long hut*
*15,000 years ago*

*Serbian hut*
*8,400 years ago*

© DIAGRAM

*Birds sing to keep other birds from their territory. Monkeys have different calls with different meanings, such as warning of a predator. Humans are unique in that they have a whole system of language designed to convey subtle meanings. When did language first begin?*

**Comparing larynx (below)**
*Unlike humans, the larynx (voice box) lies in a high position in the throat of apes.*

OUR BRAINS have two areas on the left side that are important for speech. Broca's area controls the muscles of the tongue and mouth, the mechanics of speech production. Wernicke's area is responsible for both the structure and sense of language.

In apes, there is a slight swelling where Broca's area would be situated. In fossil skulls there are signs that Broca's area became larger in the sequence *Australopithecus*; *Homo habilis*; *Homo erectus*; *Homo sapiens*. Unfortunately this does not tell us when true language evolved.

Early hominids probably made simple grunts and gestures when they communicated. A complex language could only evolve when the right structures in mouth and throat were there. In apes, the larynx (voice box) lies high in the throat. Unlike us, they can breathe and swallow at the same time. In adult modern humans, the larynx lies lower down the throat, increasing the size and flexibility of the throat as a chamber of voice production. Intriguingly, the larynx is in a high position, like a chimp, in a human baby until about 18 months old—the time at which speech begins to develop.

The skull base is arched in humans and much flatter in chimps and human infants. Can the degree of arching in fossil hominids tell us about the type of larynx they had, and whether they could talk?

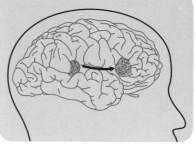

**Speech centers (above)**
*Linked centers in the left side of the brain produce swellings detectable in early fossil skulls.*

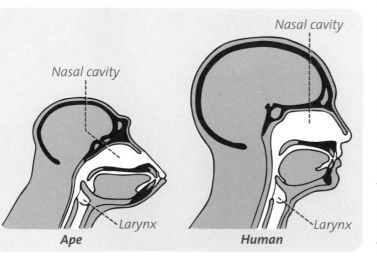

Nasal cavity

Nasal cavity

Larynx

**Ape**

Larynx

**Human**

**IT'S A FACT**
In Neanderthal people, the larynx was probably higher than ours, judging by the skull. Could this be a clue to their lack of longevity? Perhaps they could not talk to each other as well as we can today.

Australopithecines had an apelike shape. In *Homo erectus*, the larynx was probably lower, but not as low as in modern people. Speech may have been possible, but without the range of today. When *Homo sapiens* arrived, so did the low larynx, and the possibility of real speech.

Some people think that the history of toolmaking may tell us something about the history of language. *Homo erectus* made tools of a standard pattern. Did one tell the next how to do it? But the tools remained the same for a very long time. Perhaps the language was limited. *Homo sapiens* started to make a greater variety of tools. Was language also becoming more varied? With the arrival of Cro-Magnons, there was a sudden flowering of toolmaking and art. Some scientists believe that real language, in the sense we understand it, may not have started until this comparatively recent time, less than 50,000 years ago.

© DIAGRAM

*What do we know about the beliefs and thoughts of early man? We really know nothing much of the millions of years of early human history. Only once people started to leave paintings, sculptures, and other items can we begin to formulate some idea of the thoughts behind them.*

IN PREHISTORIC TIMES (as the name states) there were no written records. Experts have a few important clues about the ideas and beliefs of our early ancestors. But even they, to a large extent, have to rely on conjecture. Many mysteries also remain concerning the customs and practices of our ancestors. No one is sure, for instance, about the significance of tiny, carved figurines, known as Venuses, which have been unearthed throughout western Europe and as far east as Siberia, and the earliest are thought to be more than 30,000 years old. We can only guess that our ancestors may have been highly superstitious, and the statuettes were therefore lucky charms, fertility symbols, or perhaps representations of a mother goddess.

Some of the carved pieces known from these ancient times appear to associate animals and plants from a particular time of year. They have been interpreted as symbolic of the seasons, and perhaps used in ceremonies to mark special times of year. This is speculation from very little evidence, but this type of thinking is one of the few ways we have of trying to create a feeling for ancient ways of life.

It would appear that there has been a belief in an afterlife for many thousands of years. Even Neanderthals may have possessed such beliefs, judging by their careful burial of individuals. Later, the Cro-Magnons made ritual burials of the dead, sometimes including the things that were important for life, such as their tools, weapons, ornaments, treasures, and even food for their future use. Whatever else made up the religious beliefs held by these people is impossible to know.

## IT'S A FACT!

One South African archeologist, Professor David Lewis-Williams, has theorized that many prehistoric cave paintings found throughout the world may have been produced to represent images that came to mind either during the dreams or hypnotic trances of tribal medicine men or shamans. This is based on observations of modern San bushmen in southern Africa. However, the theory is vigorously disputed by many anthropologists. Although willing to consider ideas, many scientists believe we shall never really know what went on in the minds of men 20,000 years ago.

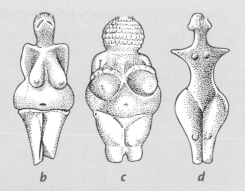

### Venus figurines
Statuettes in stone or ivory, with exaggerated female characteristics, have been found at various European prehistoric sites.
**a** France
**b** Moravia
**c** Austria
**d** Moravia

© DIAGRAM

*Early man evolved in the tropics where there was usually little need for covering the body. However, as people spread into the cooler parts of the world, wrapping the furry skin of an animal around their bodies must have made the cold nights more bearable. Gradually, as fixings and fastenings were invented, the skins were turned into clothes and even footwear. Clothes of some sort were needed in Europe and northern Asia during the Pleistocene Ice Age.*

CAVE ART depicts animals more often than humans. Portraits of people in rock art are often stylized, and are most common in areas where few clothes would be needed anyway, so there is little evidence from paintings of what early clothes were like. Some Ice Age figurines from Russia show people in what appear to be fur suits. But there is not much direct evidence of early clothes, as fur rots away over time. On the other hand, many pieces of ancient jewelry have been found. It seems that our species has enjoyed self-adornment since way back in time.

We can speculate that our ancestors came to realize the skins and furs of animals they hunted—wolves, foxes, hares, and deer, for instance—could be scraped clean of fat and wrapped round their bodies for warmth. In the later Stone Age, bone needles became common. With these needles, skins could be sewn together with rawhide or sinews and shaped into clothes.

Animal hides would also have been used to make boots to protect feet from injury while walking or hunting, and to

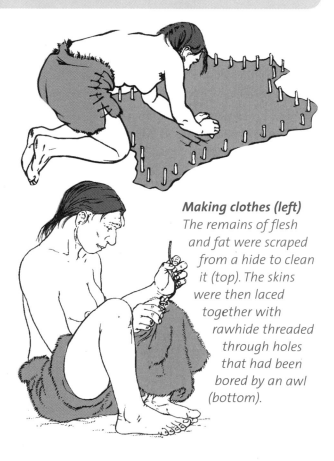

***Making clothes (left)***
*The remains of flesh and fat were scraped from a hide to clean it (top). The skins were then laced together with rawhide threaded through holes that had been bored by an awl (bottom).*

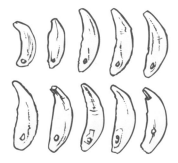

***Animal teeth (left)***
*These canine teeth had holes carefully drilled through them so they could then be strung on a necklace.*

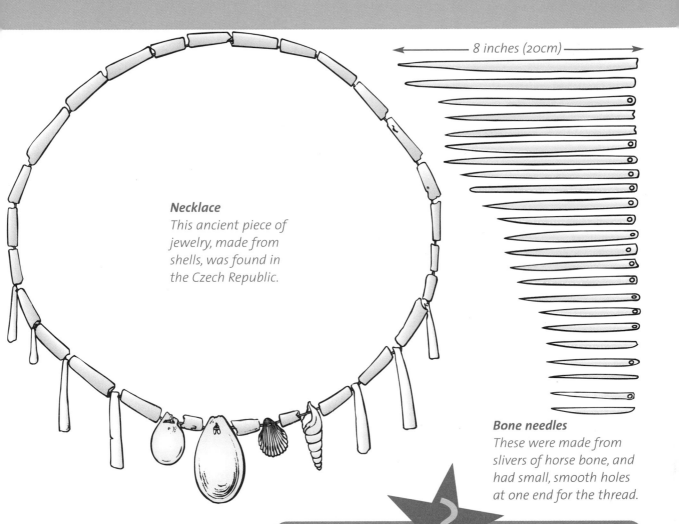

*8 inches (20cm)*

**Necklace**
*This ancient piece of jewelry, made from shells, was found in the Czech Republic.*

**Bone needles**
*These were made from slivers of horse bone, and had small, smooth holes at one end for the thread.*

keep them from freezing during winter months. In summer, grasses or reeds may have been tied to the feet to make temporary shoes.

The weaving of fabric to make into clothes was a much later development. The inspiration may have come from the making of mats and baskets from materials such as reeds and rushes.

**DID YOU KNOW?**
Some people, even today, make a sort of cloth from the bark of trees, using a technique that may well have been used by our ancestors for thousands of years. The textile produced is suitable for clothing and blankets. The bark is stripped from a tree, and the outer rind is scraped away, leaving the soft inner lining. This is soaked in water, and then hammered with stone or wooden beaters to thin the bark and give the cloth its texture.

© DIAGRAM

*Long before the invention of paper and writing, our ancestors painted cave walls with amazing depictions of wildlife. Giant deer, woolly rhinos and mammoths, wild horses, and herds of bison and aurochs (wild cattle) are just some of the many creatures that feature in the 20,000-year-old paintings that were produced by Cro-Magnon people.*

FAMOUS CAVE PAINTING sites include Altamira in northern Spain, which was discovered in 1879, and Lascaux in the Dordogne region of southwestern France, where in 1940 a group of children found the entrance to a painted cave. However, rock art is not confined to Europe; Australia's early Aborigines painted on rocks, as did people in parts of Africa.

Some of the earliest art depicting animals and people was crudely engraved on small objects but, from about 20,000 to 10,000 years ago, European cave painters left an extraordinary legacy. Many images are very realistic, reflecting their creator's eye for form and color. The artists sometimes used the shape of a cave wall to add contours, so that there would be no difficulty in seeing exactly what kind of animal was being shown. Depictions of woolly mammoths, for example, tally exactly with what is known of these extinct elephants from frozen carcasses found in the northern tundra.

In most places depictions of people are rare or absent. When they occur, they are often rather stylized. Some people left behind "negative" hand prints made by blowing pigment around a hand held to the wall. The colors of cave paintings remain fantastically vibrant today. Deep purples, blacks, sunshine yellows, and brilliant reds were obtained from natural earth pigments or charcoal, ground down and mixed with fat. People smeared color on the walls with fingers or simple sticks. "Spray" painting may have been done by taking color into

**Archer**
*A Spanish cave painting from late in the Stone Age, when bows and arrows had been invented, shows a bowman firing an arrow while holding three more.*

## DID YOU KNOW?

Although much cave art is realistic, some is difficult to understand. A painting found at Les Trois Frères, in France, appears to show a creature half stag and half human. Is it a drawing of a magician in a mask and costume, or some other creature?

*Preserving the past (below)*
*At Lascaux, an exact replica cave has been built and painted for visitors. This saves the original cave from contamination.*

## TIME MATTERS

Although many cave paintings are superb, and our ancestors seem to have been very talented artists, it is sometimes difficult to decipher the type of animal in a number of them. Whether this is because these particular depictions are not entirely accurate, or because they are the fantasies of an artist's imagination, still remains a subject of scientific debate.

© DIAGRAM

the mouth, then blowing it through pursed lips or a hollow plant stem.

We cannot be certain why the paintings were made. The animals shown were often those that were hunted. Perhaps the paintings celebrated previous hunting expeditions. Alternatively, they may have been intended as magic to conjure up successful hunting in the future. They may even have been for decoration, but this seems unlikely as in some places pictures were over-painted with new ones. Also, many paintings were deep in caves in total darkness.

The cave artists relied on primitive lamps made from slabs of stone with hollows filled with burning animal fat. This adds to our sense of wonder at the effort and skill involved. It has been suggested that special ceremonies took place in these deep caves.

*Cultural activities, such as playing music and creating art, are part of what distinguishes Homo sapiens from other species. But it is very difficult to know when humans began to make simple instruments. Some people think that we began to play music at about the time fluent speech began. Others believe that music may even have come first.*

MANY ANIMALS use sound as a means of communication. Some woodpeckers drum on tree trunks to announce their presence. Chimpanzees sometimes communicate by thumping on the huge roots of forest trees. No doubt primitive man did much the same, and drums have been used up to the present day to send messages. But this drumming is not the same as music. To create music you need different notes, and the ability to play some sort of tune.

Could stone tools have doubled up as musical instruments? We know that a modern tuned instrument can be made out of stone (a "lithophone") just as a xylophone can be made from wood. An experiment conducted at the Cincinnati Museum Center, where flints were chipped from a rock to make 100 replica flint tools, showed that it is possible to make music with them, tapping one against another. This makes distinctive wear patterns on the tool's surface. Ancient tools have been examined for similar wear. Most show none,

**The first musical instruments (below)**
*Our prehistoric ancestors developed the means for making music from a variety of raw materials.*

**Bear-bone flute (above)**
*This instrument was probably played like a recorder.*

*Bone flute (left)*
*Such flutes were used both*
*as decoy instruments, and*
*for making music.*

but a few, tantalizingly, suggest that they may have doubled up as instruments.

We know that wind instruments are very ancient. A site in China has yielded 30 prehistoric flutes, one of which is still playable. These flutes are 9,000 years old. Bone flutes found in France date back even further. Bird bones were commonly used for flutes. But the oldest flute known was dug up in Slovenia in 1995. It is made from a bear's thigh bone, and is broken, but it dates back some 53,000 years. This would make it a flute which was played by Neanderthals. Some people do not wish to credit Neanderthals with this sort of ability, and say the holes in the bone are animal bites. However, no animal bites have been identified with this sort of pattern. On the other hand, the pattern of holes will play notes on a scale, as was demonstrated by a scientist who constructed, and played, a replica.

A dig in the Ukraine unearthed instruments made from the bones of a woolly mammoth, dating back to 20,000 years ago. In all parts of the world, humans developed means of making music.

**DID YOU KNOW?**
The most ancient Hebrew instrument, still in use today during major Jewish holy days, and which produces a very strident sound, is the shofar—a ram's horn. It produces a series of notes like a bugle. Throughout the ancient world, our ancestors may have used animal horns in a similar way.

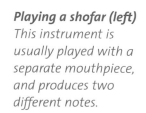

*Playing a shofar (left)*
*This instrument is*
*usually played with a*
*separate mouthpiece,*
*and produces two*
*different notes.*

© DIAGRAM

*Most of our relatives—the apes and monkeys—are social creatures that live in groups. This is likely to have been true of all the human line, from early hominids onward. But early hominids, and early "modern" humans, probably lived in small groups that were little more than a family unit. As human life became more complex, there were advantages in living in larger groups, and in having a permanent place to live.*

THE DEVELOPMENT OF SPEECH made social interaction far easier. Members of ever-larger groups could communicate, warn of danger, plan hunting tactics, and convey their feelings on a variety of subjects.

Once our ancestors had mastered the art of making fire, for cooking, warmth, and to keep wild animals from approaching, it made sense to stay in one place for a while and keep the fire going. If the place was a good one for finding food or hunting, the camp might last a long time. A group of people might return to it year after year at the same season. Archeologists think that one such site in England—at a spot called Star Carr in Yorkshire—was probably used every year for about 300 years, around 10,000 years ago, during the early summer season. About 20 people lived there. They had stone

### Tending the fire
*Stones were used to to control the potential spreading of open fires. Women would have had an important role in tending fires while men hunted.*

**Between moves**
*The forest homes of the migrant peoples of Central West Africa today resemble the impermanent structures of 10,000 years ago.*

tools and spear points made of bone and antler. They hunted deer and aurochs (wild cattle). Dogs lived with them and probably helped in the hunt.

In many places in the world there is evidence of semi-permanent camp sites. By about 10,000 years ago, though, most people in the world were shifting to a different kind of existence. Instead of being wandering hunters and gatherers of wild food, they were settling down into fixed villages. Where conditions were especially good for growing crops—in the Fertile Crescent of the Middle East (in the region of modern Iraq)—there were large numbers of settlements and some grew to be towns and even cities.

There must have been great differences in the way of life for people in different parts of the world. Not everywhere developed at the same rate. Even today, although huge cities like Tokyo and Mexico City contain tens of millions of inhabitants, there are still places, such as Namibia in southern Africa and parts of Australia, where small numbers of people live as hunter-gatherers without fixed settlements.

**DID YOU KNOW?**
One of the best-known early permanent villages was excavated at a place called Lepenski Vir in Serbia, near the Danube River. Around 8,500 years ago about 100 people lived in a group of fan-shaped wooden huts. In a central position, there is evidence of a larger hut, possibly belonging to a chief, and also a meeting place. This village is thought to have been occupied for about 800 years in total. Sculptures of human heads with fishlike expressions were also found there.

© DIAGRAM

*About 13,000 years ago, in lands just east of the Mediterranean, people were harvesting wild cereals with sickles. True agriculture, involving the purposeful planting of seeds, began to replace hunting and gathering about 10,000 years ago. Food became more readily available, and communities flourished. As a result, world population increased. However, there was a downside. If crops failed, due to lack of rainfall, or perhaps because of pests such as locusts, there was the risk of famine.*

**W**HEN DID our ancestors start to produce food and tend livestock? What sort of crops did they grow? And which animals were most widely kept?

Climate changes played their part, as the Middle East became a little wetter than before, changing from semi-desert to a grassy steppe with scattered trees. The wild grasses produced grain which was a good source of food. It may have been surprisingly easy to find enough to eat. One modern archeologist went out to cut the wild ancestor of wheat. He used a flint sickle 9,000 years old of the kind that would have been used in the first "harvests." He found he could gather 6 pounds (3 kg) of grain in an hour. In three weeks he could have gathered enough to feed a family for a year. Later, when people realized

**Harvesting wheat**
*Early farmers cut grain with a sickle (**1**, and far left), and then beat the spikes into small pieces (**2**). These bits were then tossed in a process known as winnowing (**3**) to remove unwanted pieces of straw. The grains of wheat would next be pounded to separate the grain from the husks (**4**). The grain could then be boiled into a porridge-like mixture, or ground into flour and baked into bread.*

*Reaping the grain*
*This sickle, with flint teeth,*
*was found in North Africa.*

they could sow seeds to produce even better crops, farming was underway.

The earliest real farmers we know about lived in the Fertile Crescent—an area between Egypt and the Persian Gulf—where crops, such as wheat, barley, and lentils, were grown. Later, about 7,000 years ago, people in China started to cultivate other crops, which included rice and soybeans. In Mesoamerica, 5,000 years ago, maize, beans, and squashes were in cultivation.

*Wild ancestors*
*Shown below are the ancestors of four food animals that are now found worldwide:*
*a The aurochs, domesticated 8,500 years ago, was fierce and long-horned.*
*b The wild goat, domesticated 10,000 years ago, had horns that curved straight back.*
*c The wild sheep, domesticated 11,000 years ago, with long horns.*
*d The wild boar, domesticated 9,000 years ago, with tusks, bristly coat, and long snout.*

**DID YOU KNOW?**
Just as food gathering led to farming, so hunting led to the domestication of animals. By about 8,500 years ago, some people had begun to herd cattle, sheep, and goats, and slaughtered them for food and clothing. These animals ate plants that humans found indigestible. Pigs were kept as useful scavengers and sources of meat. As yet they differed little from their ancestors, the wild boar. Selective breeding eventually produced docile animals that also gave more meat, milk, or wool as the farmer required. The keeping of such livestock is thought to have started in the Middle East, but people in other parts of the world later domesticated animals, such as llamas and alpacas in South America.

a    b    c    d

© DIAGRAM

**The Neanderthals are the first people we know of who systematically buried their dead. A number of caves have been found where they had dug holes in the floor for the burial of corpses.**

EVER SINCE THE NEANDERTHALS, burial of the dead has been common human behavior, and rituals have developed around it. As societies became more complex, with chieftains emerging, there was a tendency for people of importance to be given particularly prominent burials. Special structures, such as stone slabs or large earth mounds, were put up over their graves. Later, in civilizations such as ancient Egypt, the complex tombs of the pharaohs were so important that they might be planned and built over many years. They were often filled

*Terracotta army of Xi'an*
*This illustration shows just one section of a huge pottery army that was designed to guard the Chinese emperor in the afterlife.*

## PAST MATTERS

Stonehenge is thought to have been used in the distant past for religious ceremonies. The huge stones are carefully arranged and aligned so that they mark key points of the calendar. Some of the stones weigh as much as 28 tons (25 tonnes) and some are thought to have come from Wales, although how they were transported is not understood.

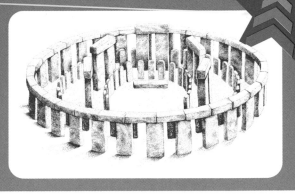

**Neanderthal burial (right)**
*This man was buried, seemingly with ceremony and reverence, about 60,000 years ago.*

**Earrings (above)**
*Careful excavation of a 4,300 year-old burial near Stonehenge yielded many interesting articles, including earrings, which suggest the body was that of a high-ranking chief.*

with treasures for the afterlife. In China emperors were also buried with great pomp, sometimes including such apparent necessities for the afterlife as the thousands-strong Terracotta Army of Xi'an! Excavations made in England during the early part of 2002, close to the mysterious prehistoric monument known as Stonehenge, revealed a remarkable Bronze Age burial. It dates from about 2,300 BCE. In it lay the skeleton of a man. When plans were drawn up to build a new school, archeologists were called in to check for Roman remains. A body buried with many precious Bronze Age belongings at his side, no doubt in the belief they would keep him safe in the life beyond, was found at the site.

Strangely, there was no sign of a burial mound, but this might have been expected as the field had often been plowed. In all, about 100 artifacts were dug up at the site, including a belt buckle, arrowheads, a bone pin, tools for butchering carcasses, copper knife blades, drinking vessels, and two magnificent gold earrings, probably worn around the lobes rather than hung from them. This evidence of wealth has led to the conclusion that the person must have been someone of influence and power. Indeed, he may well have been a king or chieftain.

© DIAGRAM

*The development of written languages is often accepted as marking the end of prehistoric times, and the start of true civilization. Written records only go back at the most 5,000 years, when writing was invented, a small fraction of the time that modern humans have existed. Writing seems to have been invented in at least three times and places: in the Middle East, China, and Mesoamerica.*

**W**RITING OFTEN SEEMS to have originated as pictographs—small stylized images of objects and animals in their surroundings. These could sometimes be strung together to make a list, or story, or suggest a particular meaning. Later, these little pictures might represent a particular sound, derived from the name of the object shown. The pictures might become even more stylized, so that they did not directly resemble the original object, but conveyed a sound, either a syllable, or the section of a word. Some modern languages are written like this. Japanese, for example, comprises syllables that can be represented by signs.

Some other languages have more sounds, and cannot conveniently be represented by syllable signs. These often developed an alphabet to represent the smaller parts from which a word is made up. English, with its Latin alphabet, and Russian, with its Cyrillic alphabet, have this type of writing system.

In Mesopotamia (the area around present-day Iraq) a form of picture writing was developed by the Sumerians over 5,000 years ago. There were some 2,000 pictures a scribe had to remember. Not surprisingly, they simplified the system, and

**Sub-Saharan rock art**
*The most characteristic sites in West Africa in which this form of art appeared were south of the Sahara between Senegal and Nigeria. This particular illustration depicts a mission in what is now known as Mali.*

ended up with a type of writing that represented the sounds of the language. They used reeds to engrave their messages on to wet clay tablets. The clay would then harden and a permanent record was created. The writing is called cuneiform (wedge-shaped) because most of the symbols were made of wedge-shaped elements.

The ancient Egyptians used a system of picture signs or hieroglyphics. Hieroglyphics were very complex, and generally appeared on the walls of tombs and buildings. With time hieroglyphics became simplified for everyday use and were written on a form of paper known as papyrus. This simplified version, or hieratic, was replaced by a version that was simpler still, known as demotic.

After the decline of ancient Egypt, the meaning of both hieroglyphics and demotic script was lost. They began to be understood again, as a result of some detective work, after the Rosetta Stone was found in 1799 near the mouth of the River Nile. This basalt stone is about 3 feet long, 2 feet wide, and 11 inches thick (90 x 60 x 28 cm) and includes 14 lines of hieroglyphics, 32 of demotic script, and 54 lines of classical Greek. From studying the Greek, scholars began to recognize words in the other two scripts.

**Tools of the trade**
*A professional scribe (right) used a pen (left), palette (top center), and a water pot (bottom center) in the practice of his art.*

**IT'S A FACT**
A script known as Linear B was used during the Greek Bronze Age about 3,500 years ago. It was first deciphered in 1953. The tablets on which this script was found provide the earliest, fully legible, examples of the written word in western civilization.

**Cuneiform writing**
*A reed pen is used to inscribe wedge-shaped characters in a soft clay tablet.*

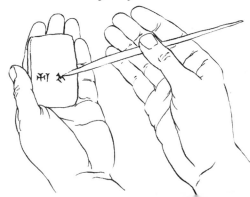

**DID YOU KNOW?**
In Mesoamerica, various civilizations developed types of writing based on pictograms. In China, writing developed over 3,500 years ago.

*It may be hard to believe, bearing in mind current concerns about global warming, but we may be in the middle of an ice age. At the moment we are probably in a relatively warm period, known as an interglacial.*

ICE AGES HAVE HAPPENED MANY TIMES in the Earth's history. There is evidence of ice age conditions some 700 million years ago, and again about 440 and 290 million years ago. The only ice age directly to affect humans is the last, Pleistocene Ice Age, which has influenced much of the last 1.7 million years. During this last period the Earth has changed back and forth from extremely cold conditions to warmer interglacials a number of times.

When the glaciations were at their height, huge areas of what is now North America, and also northern Europe and Asia, were covered with ice several miles thick. So much sea water was turned to ice that land bridges appeared where there had once been shallow seas. The dry land bridges could be crossed by migrating animals and also our ancestors. The last major glaciation began approximately 70,000 years ago, and with variations in intensity, lasted until about 12,000 years ago.

Nobody knows how these major changes in climate came about. In 1913, the Serbian scientist Milutin Milankovitch linked dramatic changes in climate occurring about every 22,000 years to alterations in the Earth's tilt. This affects the amount of sunlight reaching polar regions, and the severity of winters worldwide. A number of other factors, including circulation patterns in ocean currents, probably played a part in the development of ice ages.

*Mammoth*

During glaciations, climatic bands are shifted. Cold conditions allowed tundra (a treeless landscape with hard, frozen soil) to extend far south into Europe and America. Animals such as woolly rhinoceroses and mammoths, now extinct, lived there, as well as musk oxen, which still live in comparable areas

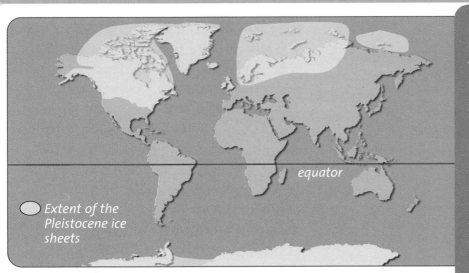

Extent of the Pleistocene ice sheets

equator

today. The Sahara was wet, but the areas of true tropical rainforest diminished. As climatic bands moved back and forth, so animals and plants were forced to shift their range. Sometimes there were barriers, such as mountains, or seas. Some extinctions, and patterns of distribution of animals and plants today, can be explained by these forced shifts.

The Ice Age is the backdrop against which the later stages of our evolution took place. Neanderthals lived in the cold European climate, as well as warmer spots. The Cro-Magnons survived and hunted surprisingly far north, in some of the worst of the Ice Age areas.

Musk ox

Woolly rhinoceros

**Ice Age mammals**
*The woolly rhinoceros, now extinct, lived across much of Europe and northern Asia. The huge, extinct cave bear lived in Ice Age Europe. The musk ox ranged across Europe, northern Asia, and America in the Ice Age, but is now found only on North American tundra.*

Cave bear

© DIAGRAM

*The whole of human history before metals were discovered and brought into use is known as the Stone Age. Virtually all tools and weapons left from this time are made from stone. Although wood and other materials were certainly used as well, they have decayed away. The Stone Age began more than two million years ago in Africa, but in the Americas it started with the first human settlers. In some parts of the world, the Stone Age ended 6,000 years ago, but in a few others it persisted until modern times. Australian aborigines and Native Americans have been able to demonstrate age-old techniques of working with stone.*

**Working with stone**
*Some modern Australian aborigines retain the skill of working stone into useful objects. This man is resting a core stone on his heel as he strikes it with a stone hammer.*

THE FIRST PART of the Stone Age is usually termed the Paleolithic ("old stone age"). This started with the first pebbles worked by *Homo habilis*, and continued through the Acheulean hand axes and other implements made by *Homo erectus*. Later still came the flake tools made by Neanderthal people, and the blades and arrowheads made by Cro-Magnon *Homo sapiens*. These are all classified as Paleolithic. The actual stone used for tools varied from place to place. Quartzite and volcanic lava were used for some early tools in Africa. Flint, rock crystal, and glassy volcanic rocks have been popular materials where they occur, as they fracture easily to give sharp edges and, although hard, they can be worked well.

The Mesolithic period ("middle stone age") is recognized in Europe from about 10,000 to 5,000 years ago. It was characterized by hunter-gatherer cultures. The Mesolithic toolbox had some new kinds of stone implements, including axes for cutting down trees. Now wood could be used not only for fires, but also to fashion dugout canoes, paddles, and even early forms of skis and sleighs with a certain degree of ease. Travel over snow and boggy ground was now possible.

The Neolithic period ("new stone age") more or less coincided with humans settling down as farmers, and was characterized by ground and polished stone tools.

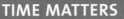

**Making a canoe**
*Flint blades (right) were used to convert a solid tree trunk into a dugout canoe (below).*

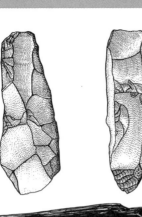

## TIME MATTERS

It was probably our late "Stone Age" ancestors who invented the bow and arrow, which made it possible to hunt at a distance. The simplest consisted of a thin piece of wood, tapered from the center to each end, and then bent into an arc by a cord shorter than the piece of wood itself. Arrowheads were simple, sharpened flints. Actual examples have been found dating from about 10,000 years ago. Rock paintings show them in use thousands of years earlier than this date.

© DIAGRAM

*About 9,000 years ago people were already experimenting with metal, making small objects out of copper. By 5,000 years ago, people had learned to mix metals in a furnace—nine parts copper to one of tin—to make what is known as bronze. This alloy (mixture of metals) is much harder than either copper or tin on their own. Bronze could be run into molds. The manufacture of weapons, such as daggers, as well as tools and decorative objects, became widespread. A new era had dawned.*

THE "BRONZE AGE" began at different times in different cultures and parts of the world. Ways of working metals may have been discovered independently several times. In Europe, the Bronze Age is one of the greatest eras of European prehistory, heralding a time of great changes, not only in people's lives, but also in technological progress through the use of this alloy. When Bronze Age settlements have been unearthed, metalwork from this period, including domestic items and jewelry, has often survived intact. Thousands of objects from this period have been found.

As well as in Europe and the Middle East, bronze was made in ancient Egypt and China. Well-developed skills and techniques with metal allowed the craftsmen to make large objects, such as doors for temples and palaces, out of bronze, as well as a range of smaller objects from spear points to cooking pots. But bronze was expensive to produce and was reserved for special objects. Most farming implements would still have been made of wood or stone.

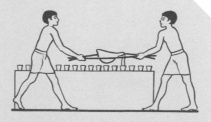

**Bronze casting in ancient Egypt**
*Workers tend a charcoal furnace (top), and then lift a crucible of molten bronze (middle), before finally pouring it into a mold to create a bronze door (bottom).*

*Tending a furnace (below)*
*An African uses bellows to push air into a bronze furnace to raise its temperature. Although Africa had no "Bronze Age," some areas, such as Benin, West Africa, had a tradition of bronze working from the 14th–19th centuries.*

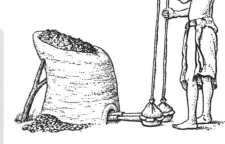

***Working with bronze***
*From ancient Egypt to medieval Europe, similar techniques were used to melt, cast, and work bronze.*

Pure copper is an unusual find, but copper ore—rock containing the metal mixed with other substances—is more common. The production of copper in quantity depended on the ability of people to recognize rocks containing copper, heat these in a furnace to 1,470°F (800°C) to melt the copper, then pour it into molds. It might then be further beaten into shape. To make bronze, tin ore must also be recognized and added to the mixture.

The Bronze Age was a time of great innovation. Oxen were harnessed to work on farms for the first time. The potter's wheel was invented and, by 5,500 years ago, the wheel was in use for transport.

***The wheel (left)***
*The Sumerians had wheeled chariots and carts 5,000 years ago. Early wheels were made of two or three pieces clamped together, and were soon rimmed with metul.*

***Bronze objects***
*Illustrations show a sword and dagger from Bronze Age Europe (top), and a Chinese cooking pot, more than 3,000 years old (bottom).*

© DIAGRAM

*Iron is a much commoner metal than copper, but it needs a much higher temperature to extract it from its ore. However, by about 3,500 years ago people had discovered how to smelt iron. The first people we know who could use this process were the Hittites, living in what is now Turkey.*

IRON ORE has to be heated at a very high temperature (2880°F, 1535°C) to melt iron. Early furnaces could not maintain this temperature reliably, and the resulting iron was often mixed with impurities which needed to be hammered out by a smith before the tool or weapon was shaped. Quenching the object in water made it harder. Carbon blended from charcoal fuel also toughened the iron, effectively making it a type of steel.

Not only is iron far commoner than copper, it is also much harder. Where it was available, iron soon took over as the metal of choice for tools and weapons, although copper and bronze might still have been important for producing decorative objects.

By 2,500 years ago, much of Asia, North Africa, and Europe were truly in the Iron Age. In China, they developed very hot furnaces which enabled pure molten iron to be used for casting objects.

In Africa south of the Sahara there was no Bronze Age, and cultures moved straight from stone to iron. There the earliest-known furnaces were in Nigeria nearly 3,000 years ago. This

*Defending the fort*
*Hill forts with large ramparts were typical of Iron Age Britain. Palisades on top of the ramparts would have improved the defense of this "castle." Defenders would have used iron spears and axes.*

**IT'S A FACT**
The idea of dividing our prehistory into Stone, Bronze, and Iron Ages was first developed by Danish scientists during the 19th century. This classification works quite well in Europe, but is less applicable in other areas. The different "Ages" may not have happened at the same time in different parts of the world. In Britain, the Iron Age lasted from about 750 BCE well into the nineteenth century.

*Smelting (below)*
*Iron ore for smelting was put into a clay furnace. Bellows were used to force air through and raise the temperature to melt the iron.*

began a long tradition of African iron-working, in which ore and finished products might be traded over long distances. People specialized as miners, smelters, or blacksmiths. Much African iron, because of the carbon that became mixed up with it in the "Iron Age" production process, was equivalent to steel, and in the 19th century was often better quality than iron goods imported from Europe.

*Shaping the metal (above)*
*Two African men make spears in the traditional way.*

© DIAGRAM

*Charles Darwin*

*Although Charles Darwin first suggested that our earliest ancestors might have originated in Africa, many European scientists were of the opinion that the human species must have evolved on their own particular continent. However, Louis Leakey and members of his family (son Richard, wife Mary, and daughter-in-law Maeve, among others) proved them to be wrong.*

ONE OF THE MOST EXCITING discoveries made by the Leakey family was claimed by Mary Leakey as the most remarkable of her career. A series of tracks made in the damp volcanic ash of an area known as Laetoli in Tanzania by three hominids were found entirely by chance in 1976. They were found on an expedition mounted with National Geographic Society support. They showed that 3.75 million years ago, a small individual, less than 5 feet (1.5 m) in height, had walked along. A smaller hominid, probably a female, had walked in his footprints, either just behind him or some time afterward. There were also signs that an even smaller hominid, probably a child, had skipped along at their side. The first positive proof that hominids had already taken to walking upright as long ago as that, half a million years earlier than previously thought, had been found, and in Africa.

Laetoli, named after the local Masai word for a particular species of red lily, had previously yielded many other hominid remains such as teeth, jaws, ribs, skulls, and leg bones; but these tracks were unique.

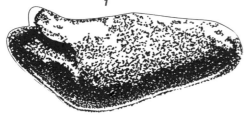

**Laetoli footprints**
*1 The original footprint which was made in newly fallen soft volcanic ash.*
*2 The contours of that footprint.*
*3 A modern human sole showing similar high and low points within the contour.*

**PAST MATTERS**

The footprints found at Laetoli provide an indication of the height and length of stride of the people who made them. They show, in addition, that at one point the smaller of the two main figures stopped, turned to the left to glance backward, almost as if to check whoever was behind was safe or that no danger lay there, and then continued in a northward direction.

*Laetoli walkers*

*The footprints at Laetoli, Tanzania, are believed to have been made by* **Australopithecus afarensis***. The walkers were fully bipedal, with big toes closely aligned with the rest of the feet.*

When the Dutch scientist Eugene Dubois suggested at the end of the 19th century that Southeast Asia might be a good place to look for early hominids, he faced mockery among the establishment. We now know, however, that he was entirely right. It was thanks to him that remains of Java Man were found. These Indonesian remains belong to the species Homo erectus. Other specimens are known from other parts of Asia. Remains of early members of our own species, Homo sapiens, are also found in Asia.

THE OLDEST of the *Homo erectus* species in Asia have been found in Java. Later Chinese specimens found near the capital, Beijing, about 360,000 years old, had a larger brain capacity than the earliest forms; these are often referred to as Peking man.

Later human skulls found at many sites in China suggest that, even as early as 100,000 years ago, people rather like those inhabiting the region today, with their characteristic wide cheekbones, had already evolved. Indeed, at as many as 15 sites all over Asia, remains have been found of fully modern humans dating from as long ago as 100,000–50,000 years.

No remains of the Neanderthal type have been found in eastern Asia. Remains unearthed at a place called Liujiang, in Kwangsi Province, China, are about 20,000 years old. They correspond exactly in their anatomy to the skeleton of a modern man from this part of the world. This suggests that

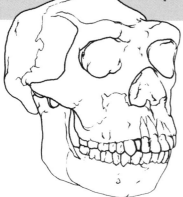

**"Pithecanthropus 4" (above)**
*This skull specimen, dating from about one million years ago, was found in Sangiran, Java.*

**Homo erectus *in Asia* (right)**
*These illustrations depict both past and present Asian examples of fully modern humans.*

*1 Quafzeh*

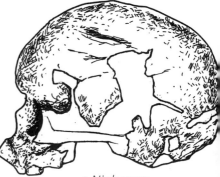

*2 Niah man*

the East Asian physical features that we see today—straight dark hair, an upper eyelid fold, a comparatively flat face, and wide cheek bones—were probably already present in people of that time.

## DID YOU KNOW?

In China, over the centuries and up until the present day, fossilized hominid bones and teeth, as well as those of various other animal species, have been dug up and ground into powder to be used as medicine for a wide variety of complaints. Scientists believe that many valuable fossils have been lost in this way.

*SOUTH CHINA SEA*

*INDIAN OCEAN*

***Where they lived (left)***
*This map shows 15 sites of finds of fully modern man from 100,000–50,000 years ago.*

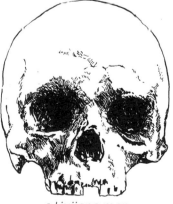

*3 Wadjak skull*          *4 Liujiang man*

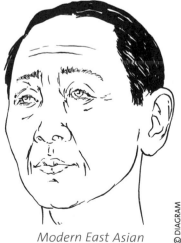

*Modern East Asian*

© DIAGRAM

Investigation of early man has been going on for longer in Europe than elsewhere. There are many specimens of early "Europeans" and their artifacts. It might be supposed that the picture of human evolution in this part of the world would be both clear and straightforward, but it is not.

**Excavated burial (above)**
Soil is brushed from a double burial, but care is taken to keep the skeletons intact.

**Cave excavation**
Precise measurements accompany the careful excavation of limestone fissures bearing valuable fossil fragments.

IT IS NOT REALLY SURPRISING that we still cannot tell a straightforward story about evolution in Europe. Many of the remains that are found are very fragmentary, and just tiny samples of ancient populations. There have been tremendous variations in the conditions in Europe during some of the times it has been inhabited by humans, and presumably they adapted accordingly. At times, caribou have roamed southern Europe, but at others, humans may have encountered lions and hippopotamuses there.

Probably three main types of human have inhabited Europe: *Homo erectus*, who left behind pear-shaped hand axes; Neanderthals; and modern *Homo sapiens*. Some of the fossils could be seen as intermediate types. A fossil from near London, England, called "Swanscombe Man," is about 250,000 years old. The remains consist of a skullcap, probably female, with some old-fashioned characteristics, but fairly similar to modern people. Some people have seen it as ancient *Homo sapiens*, while others have emphasized ways in which it resembles Neanderthals. This person lived alongside lions, elephants, and rhinoceroses. Swanscombe Man probably had a brain size similar to ours. In Steinheim, Germany, a 300,000-year-old skull was discovered with a slightly smaller brain but, again, it could be classified as either Neanderthal or very early *Homo sapiens*, as might the jaw known as Heidelberg Man, or *Homo heidelbergensis*.

Neanderthals remain mysterious. How close are they to us? DNA testing on their bones suggests they were so different that they are not our ancestors, but possibly a separate species. Some fossils, though, have characteristics between the Neanderthal species and modern humans. Did Neanderthals give rise to modern people after all? Did they interbreed to produce hybrids of mixed character? There is plenty still to discover, and many possible relationships to unravel.

## PAST MATTERS

We are not even sure when Neanderthals died out. It used to be thought that they disappeared about 35,000 years ago, but recent testing of Neanderthal bones from Croatia have given a date of 28,000 years ago, when modern humans were certainly living nearby. Bones from Portugal suggest that Neanderthals (or Neanderthal-modern hybrids) may still have been living there 25,000 years ago.

© DIAGRAM

**Rebuilding a skull**
*The anatomist arranges bones around a soft clay, model head, and then reshapes this to match the curves of the assembled skull.*

*The first settlers in North and South America were immigrants from Asia who moved there during the Ice Age.*

THE FIRST HUMANS had crossed in several waves from Siberia to Alaska some time between 35,000 and 15,000 years ago. They walked over a stretch of land which is now covered by the sea of the Bering Strait. They moved southward, probably funneled along particular routes, because of glaciers covering mountains, such as the Rockies. They fanned out across the Great Plains, and ever southward through Central and South America, right down to Patagonia, now in Argentina, and eventually to Tierra del Fuego at the southern tip of the continent. One expert has calculated that if a single hunting group started from the Bering Strait and moved its camp just three miles southward every week, in theory it could have reached the very tip of South America in 70 years. Of course, several new generations would have been born by then and, in favorable conditions, it would take only a small number of generations for an originally small hunting group to increase its population to many thousands.

With their origins in Asia, it is not surprising that the descendants of these people throughout the Americas have

**Artifacts (above)**
*Typical items include: a clovis point (top) fixed to a shaft (about 12,000 years old); and a hide scraper (bottom) made of bone with a serrated end (only 1,800 years old).*

**Aboriginal Americans**
*An Inuit (left), a Dakota Indian (center), and a child from Tierra del Fuego, South America (right), are shown below.*

**Pre-Columbian life (left)**
*Different ways of life dominated in different parts of the Americas:*
*a Mainly hunting and fishing;*
*b Farming with some hunting;*
*c Gathering, and hunting;*
*d Mexican civilization;*
*e Olmec civilization;*
*f Mayan civilization; and*
*g Inca empire.*

**Portrait vase (right)**
*This was made by the Mohica, a rich culture from the northern coast of Peru (200 BCE–600 CE).*

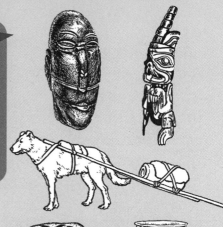

characteristics in common with East Asians. Straight black hair, dark eyes, wide cheekbones, and shovel-shaped incisor teeth are typical. The facial features of someone from the tip of South America today has a marked resemblance to someone of Chinese extraction.

Debate continues as to when these people arrived. The recent redating of one particular skull found in California, and known as Del Mar man, once thought to have been 48,000 years old but now believed to be less than 12,000 years old, for example, has cast doubt on the theories of those who believe these settlers arrived at a far earlier date.

Finds at the Yukon's Old Crow Basin, including a 1,800-year-old scraper for animal hides, and remains found at a site in Chile from 12,500 years ago, support the view that *Homo sapiens* came to the Americas between those dates. We also know that our species had certainly arrived by 12,000 years ago from the distinctive stone spearheads, called clovis points, found as far apart as Mexico and Alaska.

*Pre-Columbian objects*
*These include (from the top, and left to right): an Inuit carved head in ivory; a spoon handle by northwest-coast Indians; a dog-hauled pole-sled from Great Plains Indians; a birch bark box from eastern woodlands; a jar from Arizona; an Olmec carved head; a painting of the maize god by the Maya; and (below) a gold llama made by the Incas.*

© DIAGRAM

*James Cook, the British explorer, was the leader of the 18th-century expedition which "discovered" Australia. However, people had already been living there for thousands of years before this particular event.*

Paleoanthropologists have calculated from fossilized remains and tools that there were human beings in Australia at least 60,000 years ago, and perhaps for much longer. The first of these settlers arrived from Southeast Asia on rafts and in canoes at a time when the sea level was considerably lower than it is today. Many islands then formed single landmasses so that there were not broad stretches of ocean to cross.

Not all of these arrivals looked like the aborigines of today. Some skeletal remains, dating from 30,000 years ago, belong to people who were very slightly built, and may have had much in common with present-day southern Chinese. Bones found later, though, are similar to the Australian aborigines of today.

Until recently, some aborigines continued to live in a very undeveloped culture, in some ways similar to Stone Age period cultures elsewhere in the world. Although many of the tribes and groups lived within a particular area that they knew well, they might have been semi-nomadic, making use of different parts of their range as the seasons changed, when different plants and animals were available as food. Although these people wore little clothing, used spears and boomerangs to hunt, and painted their bodies with decorative designs, this does not mean they were not able to survive in a modern environment. Their knowledge of wild foods, and their memory of where to find them, would put many so-called "civilized" people to shame.

Modern meteorologists have realized that it might be worth tapping aborigine knowledge of the seasons and weather signs to help their own scientific data.

Aborigines never seem to have used the bow and arrow. Perhaps for upright animals hunted for food, such as a kangaroo in open country, the boomerang and spear with throwing stick are quite efficient enough. Not that all early Australians lived in open country. Some groups lived in and used the northern rainforest.

### Hunters (above)
Aborigines use spears for hunting, and also curved sticks called boomerangs. Hunting boomerangs usually fly straight to the target, and are not built to return.

### Dancers (below)
These illustrations show human figures drawn on rocks in northern Australia.

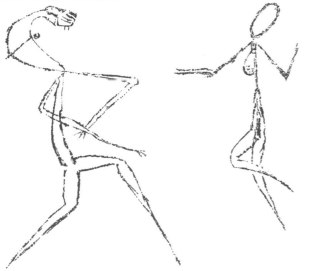

## DID YOU KNOW?
Aboriginal rock art has a long tradition, and some of the paintings may predate those found in famous French and Spanish caves. As well as being of interest in themselves, aboriginal customs and traditions may shed light on Stone Age practices in other parts of the world.

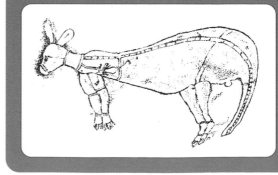

© DIAGRAM

*One of the most renowned but controversial paleontologists of the 20th century was Raymond Dart (1893–1988). He was born in Australia, but made several important discoveries while working in South Africa.*

IN 1924, RAYMOND DART discovered a small skull at a place called Taung, near Kimberley in South Africa. It was so small that it became known as the Taung baby although it was actually between four and six years old. It had a braincase the size of an ape's. Many of its features, however, were distinctly human, particularly the teeth and the shape of the face. It also seemed that the skull would have belonged to a creature that walked upright rather than on all fours.

*Fossil finders*

*Many people added to our knowledge of early humans. Here are just some of them:*

**1 Jacques Boucher de Perthes** *(1788–1868)*
*He found hand axes in France, and suggested that humans had a long prehistory.*

**2 John Lloyd Stephens** *(1805–1852)*
*He pioneered archeology in Central America.*

**3 Augustus Pitt-Rivers** *(1827–1900)*
*He brought in modern archeological techniques.*

**4 Eugene Dubois** *(1858–1940)*
*He discovered Homo erectus.*

**5 Robert Broom** *(1866–1951)*
*He discovered australopithecine remains including Australopithecus africanus.*

**6 Franz Weidenreich** *(1873–1948)*
*He made reconstructions of Peking Man.*

**7 Gustav von Koenigswald** *(1902–1982)*
*He made Homo erectus discoveries in Java.*

**8 Louis Leakey** *(1903–1972)*
*He discovered early human fossils in East Africa.*

**9 Mary Leakey** *(1913–1996)*
*She discovered Australopithecus boisei, and her expedition found the famous Laetoli footprints.*

**10 Donald Johanson** *(1943–)*
*He found Australopithecus afarensis—"Lucy."*

1

2

6

7

Dart considered the skull could have been up to two million years old, but for a long time other scientists would not accept this. What boosted Dart's confidence, however, was an idea put forward by Charles Darwin in the 19th century. In his book *The Ascent of Man*, Darwin had suggested that the place to look for human origins would be Africa.

Raymond Dart was actually criticized at the time by the scientific establishment for, among other things, coining the name *Australopithecus*. The word itself means "southern ape," but is a mixture of Latin and Greek, which was thought to be an unsuitable combination at the time.

**DID YOU KNOW?**
Raymond Dart's discoveries are now generally recognized as having revolutionized the study of human evolution. Indeed, his unearthing of the Taung skull showed that an upright way of walking preceded the development of a larger brain.

3

4

5

***Kamoya Kimeu***
*He worked alongside the Leakeys, the renowned Anglo-Kenyan family of anthropologists. Kimeu was well known for his ability to uncover the tiniest fossil fragments and, in 1984, he discovered a 1.5 million-year-old* Homo erectus *skeleton near Lake Turkana, Kenya, East Africa.*

8
9
10

*Imagine the excitement! Over 90 years ago, paleoanthropologists thought they had come up trumps and discovered the missing link between humans and apes. But all was not as it seemed.*

IN 1912, THE GEOLOGICAL DEPARTMENT of London's British Museum announced to a fascinated public that it would soon be putting on display the fossilized skull of the oldest known inhabitant of Great Britain, and perhaps the whole of Europe, which had been unearthed in a gravel pit at Piltdown Common, Sussex, England. It was thought to date back hundreds of thousands of years. It was found by an attorney, Charles Dawson, who collected fossils as a hobby. The new species was named after him, *Eoanthropus dawsoni*.

Right from the start, some experts were skeptical. A number of scientists even went so far as to suggest the remains might be fraudulent. However, the remains appeared to confirm a theory current at the time that the development of a large brain came before facial changes in human history. Piltdown man appeared to have an apelike face, but a brain case at least twice the size of any known ape's.

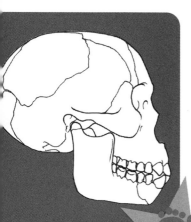

**IDENTIKIT**
The reconstruction of the Piltdown skull resembles an australopithecine, something that was not to be discovered for another 20 years. However, although the jaw sticks out (unsurprisingly, as it is an ape's) the skull and braincase are those of a modern man.

*Unearthing the remains*
*Workmen helped Charles Dawson to uncover many animal fossils at Piltdown Common. Some of those associated with Piltdown man are now suspected of being smuggled onto the site, perhaps like the "man" himself.*

For a long time, the remains were shut away, making it difficult for scientists to study them, except through plaster casts made from the original. Finally, the doubters were allowed access to test the remains. They used one of the most reliable dating methods of the time to compare the amount of mineral fluoride in the skull with the amount in the surrounding deposits. If the skull and surrounding gravel were of the same age, they would contain the same quantity of fluoride from groundwater. As it turned out, they did not, causing pandemonium in the scientific world.

The remains were shown to be fakes in 1953. To this day no one is certain who carried out this splendid hoax. Suggestions included Charles Dawson himself and the British anatomist, Arthur Keith. Whoever the guilty party may have been, he or she certainly had a sense of humor.

## IT'S A FACT
Piltdown man, when examined closely, consisted of two quite different parts. The skull of a human no more than 500 years old had been stained to produce the effect of great age. The jawbone of an orangutan, with its teeth shaped by filing, had been cleverly matched for size, and similarly aged. Even many experts were fooled.

*Examining the evidence*
*A group of scientists examine the Piltdown remains in 1915. Arthur Keith is shown seated in the white coat, while Charles Dawson stands behind to his left.*

© DIAGRAM

*The Hadar region of Ethiopia is extremely hot and desolate, but it has also proved to be a treasure house of ancient remains. In this very place a young paleoanthropologist was to make one of the most dramatic discoveries of the last century.*

THE ANCIENT LAKE SEDIMENTS OF HADAR, dating back to between three to four million years ago, are about 100 miles (160 km) northeast of Ethiopia's capital, Addis Ababa. There seemed a good chance that human remains might exist in this area. So Donald Johanson set out in 1974 to explore the area in an attempt to find evidence of early hominids. A few months later, he discovered the fossilized bones of "Lucy," a tiny hominid whose species later became known as *Australopithecus afarensis*, after the name of the African region where she was unearthed.

Hadar has been described as a wasteland of rock, gravel, and sand. Fortunately almost all the fossils found there are exposed on the surface of the ground. It hardly ever rains there; when it does, water roars down gullies and reveals more fossilized remains. While out on a dig with some local people on that lucky day in 1974, a gut feeling made Johanson work a little longer and take a small detour. Soon they spotted "Lucy's" remains—first part of her arm, then the back of her skull, then her thighbone.

Later that day, everyone on the expedition prepared to look for more of Lucy's skeletal remains, a task which ultimately took three weeks. In all, finally, there were hundreds of pieces of bone, making up about 40 percent of a complete skeleton. There was no bone duplication, so Johanson was now certain that these were the remains of a single individual.

As Johanson said:

*"Hadar is a big place, and there is a tremendous amount to do. If I had waited another few years, the next rains might have washed away many of her bones down the gully. They would have been lost, or at least badly scattered; it would not have been possible to establish that they belonged together. What was utterly fantastic was that she had come to the surface recently, probably in the last year or two. Five years earlier, she would have been buried. Five years later, she would have been gone."*

**A scientist at work**
*Johanson holds up a fragment of newly-discovered bone (top), and later cleans his finds with great care back in the protection of his field laboratory (bottom).*

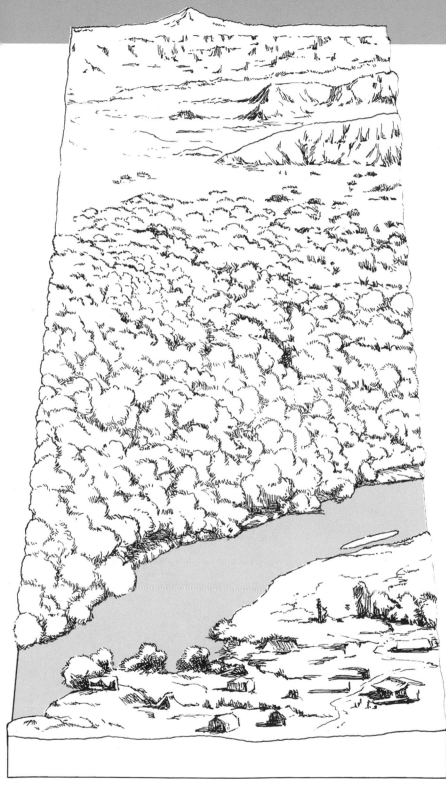

**DID YOU KNOW?**
Since 1974, other australopithecines have also been found in the Hadar area, among them a whole "family" of 13 people that had died at the same time.

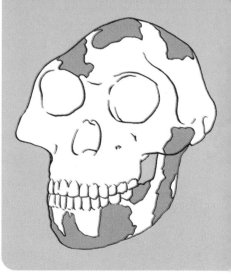

*Lucy's skull (above)*
*This is a realistic reconstruction of Lucy's skull. The darker fragments are the parts that were actually found.*

*A place to camp (left)*
*In the middle of harsh and dry countryside, a river provides running water for Johanson's expedition.*

*In 1991, two German walkers high in the Alps near the border between Austria and Italy saw a man's body emerging from the ice. Thinking he was a fairly recent casualty, perhaps lost in a winter storm, they called for help. To begin with, nobody realized that they were dealing with an amazingly preserved Neolithic Age man, complete with clothes and tools.*

THE ICEMAN, OR "OETZI" as he has been named, actually died about 5,300 years ago, and had been frozen and dried by the weather in the high mountains. He was slightly damaged by his removal from the ice before his importance was realized. Even so, an enormous amount has already been discovered by studying him and, many years after his emergence from the ice, new facts are emerging.

Oetzi was about 5 feet 5 inches (1.65 m) tall, had black hair, and was probably about 45 years old. He had arthritis, was infested with worms, and had broken ribs. He had eaten ibex meat and wheat shortly before death. He had lived somewhere

**The iceman's possessions**
*Shown below is a selection of objects which were found with the corpse of Oetzi:*

1 *An unstrung bow;*
2 *Some arrows;*
3 *A deerskin quiver;*
4 *A flint-bladed knife;*
5 *A needle-pointed bone awl, and grass string;*
6 *Mushrooms threaded on a leather string;*
7 *A deer-antler-and-wood tool, which may have been used to sharpen the knife blade.*

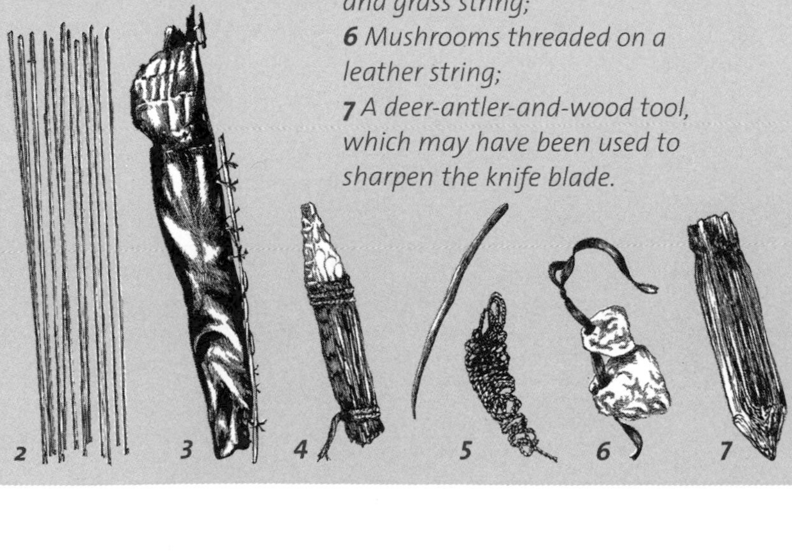

where copper was smelted, judging by the copper and arsenic levels in his hair.

The iceman's clothes were well preserved. He had a cap of bearskin, and a jacket made of goat and deerskin sewn together with sinews. He had leather trousers, and a cape woven from grass. On his feet were leather shoes, padded with grass for the rough ground. He had a rucksack of leather on a frame of larch and hazel wood.

In a small leather pouch Oetzi carried some flints, a needle, and string plaited from grass. On a string were two mushrooms, which may have been useful as an antiseptic.

He was carrying a 6-foot-long (1.8 m) bow made of yew, but it was obviously new, and needed work, including stringing, to make it serviceable. A quiver of deerskin held 14 arrows, but only two were equipped with flight feathers. He had a small knife, made of flint with an ash wood handle, that was held in a woven grass sheath. Last, but not least, was an axe with a copper blade that had obviously seen use. It had an L-shaped handle of yew wood.

**A grave discovery**
*Two German Alpine walkers on the verge of discovering the preserved body of a Neolithic Age man.*

**STRANGE BUT TRUE**
For a long time it was thought that the iceman had perished because he was caught up in a sudden blizzard and froze to death. In 2001, though, X-rays revealed an arrowhead buried in his shoulder. He died from his wounds after being shot, although he probably escaped after the attack, as none of his valuable equipment was taken. In 2003, traces of blood on his clothes and weapons were analyzed, and were found to come from four other people. Had he killed or wounded them in a fight just before his own death?

© DIAGRAM

In 1941, during World War II, irreplaceable remains of the ancient hominid Peking man were lost as they were being taken from China to the United States, theoretically for safekeeping.

DURING THE 1920s, a number of prehistoric teeth and fossilized bones were dug up in a cave at a place called Dragon Bone Hill near Peking (now Beijing), the capital of China, showing that ancient humans lived this far north on the continent of Asia 360,000 years ago. Originally called *Sinanthropus*, these remains were soon seen to have a great resemblance to Java man, called *Pithecanthropus* at the time. Now both these forms of early man are placed, together with others from elsewhere in the world, in the species *Homo erectus*. The first reasonably complete skull was found in 1929, and excavations continued in the 1930s. In the same decade China and Japan became locked in a long war. In 1937, excavations ceased, but bones from 45 individuals of the Peking man species had already been found. Peking man lived in cool conditions, and kept warm in the caves using fire. Although similar to Java man, these later examples of

**Bust of Peking man**
*The fossil remains were lost during World War II, but we still have plaster casts and reconstructions of the originals.*

*Homo erectus* from Peking had larger brains. Casts were made of at least some of the fossils for study by scientists and also for display purposes.

A lot more could probably have been gathered from careful examination of the fossils. In 1941, however, the war between China and Japan reached crisis point. The Chinese became very concerned about the Peking man remains in case a bomb chanced to drop on them. They decided to send them to the United States for safekeeping and further study. As things turned out, they could not have made a worse decision: the American marines entrusted with the task of transporting the fossils by train to a Chinese port for shipment to the United States were captured by the Japanese and sent to prison camps; their equipment and munitions were seized; and the fossils were never seen again.

Luckily, the plaster casts made of the fossils still remain in some museums, but these cannot give the range of information that might be available, with modern methods, if the original fossil bones and teeth were still available.

**DID YOU KNOW?**
The classic, first Peking man specimens may have been lost, but other remains have been found since nearby, and also in other parts of China.

**The bone collectors (above)**
*Dr W.C. Pei, together with colleagues from Canada and the United States, found the first almost complete Peking man skull in 1929.*

**Dragon bones (left)**
*These fossilized animal teeth were ground into powder for Chinese medicine.*

© DIAGRAM

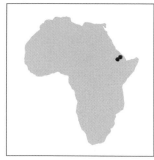
*Afar, Ethiopia*

LIKE OTHER ANIMALS, each type of hominid that we believe is a separate species is given a scientific name. This consists of two parts. The first is the genus to which it belongs (it may share this name with its closest relations), and is always written with a capital letter. The second name is the species name, and always starts with a small letter, even if it is named after some place or somebody. The genus and species name together pin the species down. Scientific names used to be derived from Latin. Nowadays they may not be, but are "Latinized" to fit the system.

Some hominid names are given below, together with their meanings and pronunciation (in brackets). The stressed syllable is underlined.

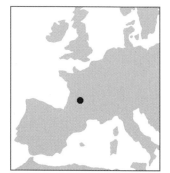
*Cro-Magnon, France*

*Australopithecus afarensis* (<u>owst</u>-ral-oh-<u>pith</u>-ek-us af-ar-<u>en</u>-sis) "southern ape from Afar"—named after the region where these remains were first found, Afar, in Ethiopia, Africa.

*Australopithecus africanus* (<u>owst</u>-ral-oh-<u>pith</u>-ek-us af-rik-<u>ahn</u>-us) "southern ape from Africa"—named after the continent, Africa, where the remains were first found.

*Australopithecus boisei* (<u>owst</u>-ral-oh-<u>pith</u>-ek-us <u>boy</u>-say-ee) "southern ape"—named after Charles Boise, a London businessman who sponsored the expedition during which the remains of this hominid were first found.

*Australopithecus robustus* (<u>owst</u>-ral-oh-<u>pith</u>-ek-us roh-<u>bust</u>-us) "robust southern ape"—named because of its strong build.

*Cro-Magnon* (<u>kroh</u>-man-yon)—named after the cave in France where remains were first found.

*Hominid*—a creature belonging to the family Hominidae, to which humans belong.

Australopithecus boisei

*Homo erectus* (<u>hoh</u>-moh er-<u>ek</u>-tus) "upright man"—named because of its upright stance.

*Homo habilis* (<u>hoh</u>-moh <u>hab</u>-il-is) "handy man"—named for its supposed dexterity when using tools.

*Homo sapiens* (<u>hoh</u>-moh <u>sap</u>-ee-enz) "wise man," is our own species. We named ourselves to emphasize our intelligence.

*Homo sapiens sapiens* (<u>hoh</u>-moh <u>sap</u>-ee-enz <u>sap</u>-ee-enz)—a name given to the modern species of human to distinguish it from Neanderthal man. Some people used to think modern man and Neanderthal man were both sub-species of the species *Homo sapiens* but that now seems to be unlikely.

*Java man*—a type of *Homo erectus*, found on the island of Java, Indonesia.

*Neanderthal man*—now usually designated *Homo neanderthalensis* (<u>hoh</u>-moh nee-<u>and</u>-er-tal-<u>en</u>-sis) "man from the Neander Valley." It was named after the place where remains were first unearthed.

*Nutcracker man*—a nickname of *Australopithecus boisei*, which had enormous jaws.

*Peking man*—a type of *Homo erectus*, found near Peking, China.

*Pithecanthropus* (pith-ee-can-throw-pus) "ape man"—an old name for Java man.

*Ramapithecus* (ram-a pith-ek-us) "Rama's ape"—named after the Hindu god, Rama.

*Sinanthropus* (sigh-nan-throw-pus) "Chinese man"—an old name for Peking man.

*Sivapithecus* (siv-a-<u>pith</u>-ek-us) "Siva's ape"—named after the Hindu god, Siva or Shiva.

*Neander valley, Germany*

1 Peking, China
2 Java, Indonesia

*Siva Nataraja*

© DIAGRAM

*A passion for retrieving information; detective ability; great attention to detail; a liking for working outdoors some of the time; infinite patience; the ability to work as part of a team—these are just some characteristics that make an individual successful at finding and interpreting fossils, particularly those of early man.*

THE ROCKS THAT CONTAIN REMAINS of early man are relatively young, from the last five million years or less, and many are comparatively soft. In several parts of Africa, for example, the rocks are wearing away at their surfaces with the action of wind and rain.

In these places it may be possible to find fossils simply by walking across the surface using sharp eyes to detect fossils. In other places, such as Olduvai, a gorge has formed that cuts down through layers of earth going back millions of years. This gives access to these layers, and the chance to spot any fossils that are weathering out. Lake shores, quarries, and even road cuttings may be good places to start looking for fossils.

Finding the first fragment is just part of the story. Are any other parts close by? How are they positioned in relation to each other? A great deal of information

**Losing the evidence**
*Ancient human fossils are seldom found intact. For example, hyenas and vultures may have dismembered the dead hominid (left); and floods may then have shed layers of fine sediment upon the isolated fragments of human bone (center). Exposed by a river's migration across its flood plain, this skull endured more weathering before its final discovery (below).*

about the conditions when a fossil formed may be deduced from the way the parts are set in the ground.

Gone are the days when a specimen was just grabbed from the ground and triumphantly taken to the laboratory. In modern times, the fossils will be photographed before removal, and each stage of the excavation will be recorded. Everything will be measured, and on a large site, whether it holds very early man, or more recent archeological remains, the whole area may be divided into a grid to help pinpoint positions.

The initial breaking up of covering earth may be done with picks and shovels, then smaller tools. Any finds, such as bones and teeth, may be cleared with brushes and fine dental tools. Finally the finds are lifted. They may need coating with a protective glaze, or even a plaster coat, for transportation to a laboratory.

*Hunting fossil hominids*

*A group of hunters scouts weathered stones that litter a landscape in East Africa for small objects of unusual shape or color which may be fossil remains of our ancestors. Fossil human bone is sometimes white or gray, but can also be black, and usually turns up in the form of isolated fragments.*

## DID YOU KNOW?

Fossils of early man are not common. In Africa, one six-person expedition spent 11 years, and found an average of three fossils per year per person, combing hundreds of square miles (km²). Most of these were only bone fragments, or single teeth.

© DIAGRAM

*Bringing a fossil to the laboratory is not the end of the story. In fact, much of the hard work may just be beginning. The fossil may need cleaning, or further preparation to remove adhering earth or rock. If it is a fragment, it may need to be assembled together with other fragments before the whole body can be understood.*

A FOSSIL MAY BE WORKED AT by tiny drills and needles to tease off the remains of the rock in which it was embedded. For tiny fossils, it may be necessary to work under a binocular microscope. All the while, the worker must avoid damaging the fossil, or adding scratches and marks that will obscure any that may be there naturally in the specimen, as the latter may provide insight into the fossil's role in life, or what happened to it after death.

Some fossils are encased in a limestone matrix. They may be released by repeated dipping in acetic acid (vinegar) which will gradually dissolve the rock. Fragile bones can be treated with

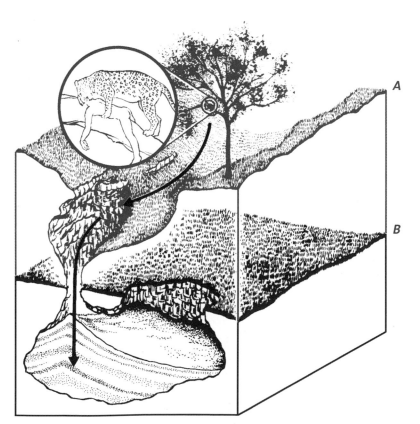

**Putting the pieces together**
*The telltale holes in the top of a* Australopithecus robustus *skull match the lower canines of a leopard (above). One possible scenario as to what happened could be as follows. Having killed its prey, the leopard then drags the corpse up a tree out of the reach of hyenas. The hominid bones then drop into a limestone fissure, and are then covered by layers of sediment (left). They lie there until discovered by a fossil hunter thousands of years later.*
**A** *Old land level*
**B** *Present land level*

chemicals that will harden and preserve them. Teeth are usually in relatively good condition as they are the hardest tissue in the body.

Much anatomical skill is required to piece together a broken and incomplete skeleton. Some matters are relatively straightforward. If the left hand of a hominid is present, we can be fairly sure what the right hand looked like. Obviously, the more there is of a skeleton, the more correct guesses will be about the remaining parts. However, many remains of early hominids are so fragmentary that we may be left in the dark about quite large parts of their anatomy. These must be inferred from other specimens, related species, and so on. Not until the time of the Neanderthals—with the one notable exception of an almost complete 1.5 million-year-old skeleton found at Lake Turkana in Africa—are we ever dealing with whole skeletons.

The reconstruction of soft parts is even more conjectural. Nobody has seen the skin and eye colors of Neanderthals, let alone the much earlier forms of human. If we have enough skeleton we can work out how muscular they were, but not how hairy. Most of the drawings and models of early man must contain a degree of artistic imagination in their depiction. Nevertheless, there is great skill and a great deal of real information put into most attempts at reconstructions.

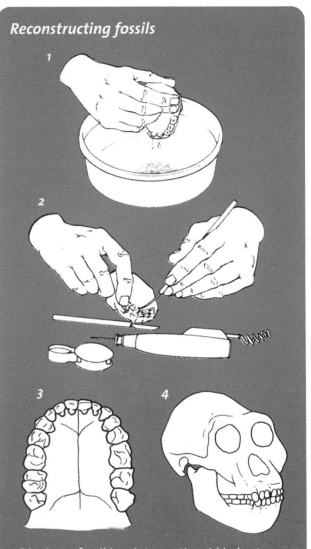

**Reconstructing fossils**

1 Dipping a fossil jaw into acetic acid helps to dissolve any adhering rock.
2 Dental picks, vibrating tools, scalpels, and magnifying lenses are used to free a fossil from its matrix.
3 Tooth rows are reconstructed which can provide a clue as to the identity of the deceased hominid.
4 A skull can be reconstructed using the tooth row as a starting point, and then adding any other available matching skull fragments.

*Nobody took a census at the time of the Neanderthals, but scientists calculate that, if there had been one, it is unlikely that the count would add up to more than a million individuals. Yet now* Homo sapiens *is numbered in billions.*

**W**E CANNOT KNOW for sure how many hominids populated the world at various stages of our history, but experts can hazard a guess. Two million years ago there may have been a million australopithecines living in Africa, although we cannot be sure. It is thought that 10,000 years ago, by which time *Homo sapiens* had colonized most of the world, there were 10 million of us at the most. The hunter-gatherer lifestyle of people back then meant that each person needed a large area to sustain them, and this placed limits on the population. Life was hard, and mortality from disease, injury, and starvation removed many from the population, often when they were still quite young.

By 7,000 years ago, farming had begun to produce a greater food supply. The diet was not necessarily better, but there was food for a greater number of people. More survived to become

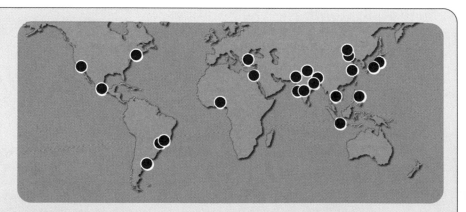

*Growth of the megalopolises*
*By 2015 there will be 23 cities with a population of over 10 million people. Moreover, five of these will have over 20 million people.*

**Population (in millions)**

| | | | |
|---|---|---|---|
| Tokyo 26.4 | Karachi 19.2 | Metro Manila 14.8 | Beijing 12.3 |
| Mumbai (Bombay) 26.1 | Mexico City 19.2 | Shanghai 14.6 | Rio de Janeiro 11.9 |
| Lagos 23.2 | New York City 17.4 | Los Angeles 14.1 | Osaka 11.0 |
| Dhaka 21.1 | Jakarta 17.3 | Buenos Aires 14.1 | Tianjin 10.7 |
| São Paulo 20.4 | Kolkata (Calcutta) 17.3 | Cairo 13.8 | Hyderabad 10.5 |
| | Delhi 16.8 | Istanbul 12.5 | Bangkok 10.1 |

adults, these produced new generations, and population growth had begun. By 1 CE, the time of the Roman emperor Augustus, there were probably 300 million people. Since then, wars or famine in some areas temporarily reduced numbers, and epidemics such as plague wiped out a large segment of the population, but the growth trend has been upward.

The pressure to find more living space, more housing, and to produce more from agriculture, is enormous. The conundrum is how to provide for the Earth's people without destroying the environment and its future capacity to provide. Worldwide, the 20th century saw a huge rise in urban dwelling. Even in the developing world, more and more people are nowadays drawn to cities to earn a living.

## IT'S A FACT
Back in the 18th century, Thomas Malthus claimed that population had the potential to grow much faster than food supply, and that this could end in universal starvation. However, in the 19th century, and still more in the 20th, modern techniques have increased food supply more than Malthus could ever envisage.

**"Super rice" (above)**
*Agricultural scientists are constantly searching for new ways to grow plants that yield more food content. "Super rice" (right) produces more rice grains than both the traditional rice (left) and the rice types of the Green Revolution of recent years (center).*

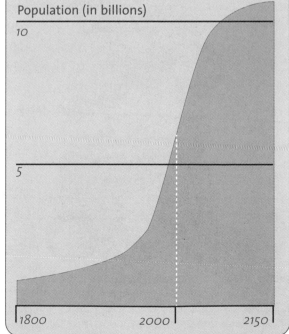

**Population growth (below)**
*At the start of the 19th century, the world population was about one billion, and reached six billion at the end of the millennium. On present trends, the population will reach 10 billion by 2150.*

Population (in billions)

10

5

1800    2000    2150

© DIAGRAM

*Most species, scientists calculate, last no more than three million years. Will Homo sapiens face a similar fate? Will humans last even that long, as more and more crowd the planet? It is interesting to speculate on our future. However, we will probably be wrong.*

**F**IFTY YEARS AGO, many stories and comics set in the "future"—that is, the year 2000 onward —depicted space travel as being routine, and the world populated by healthy and attractive individuals who had an orderly system of world government. As we know, life has not yet caught up with this image. In spite of enormous changes and advances in some respects, the human condition is far from utopian, and for the majority of the world's population, life is very hard indeed.

Today, at least one quarter of the world is seriously undernourished and one tenth is actually on the verge of starvation. The world produces sufficient food for everyone living at present, but it is unevenly distributed. Wealthier countries may produce too much and sometimes destroy huge quantities of food that cannot be used locally, to maintain prices. Poor countries may not be able to feed their own citizens. The problem is sometimes made worse by rich countries buying produce from the poor countries grown on land that might be put to better use feeding the poor countries' own populations.

Even where food is plentiful, there are problems. In some parts of the developed world, in particular the United States, but increasingly in parts of Europe, people have so much food to choose from that they are eating too much. Together with a

*Species under threat*
*The rapid growth of the human population has corresponded to the decline of many other species. Human greed for land, and other natural resources, has resulted in a threat to almost every other form of life inhabiting the Earth.*

| Number of species threatened, by group | | | | | | | | |
|---|---|---|---|---|---|---|---|---|
| 30,800 | 1,183 | 1,130 | 938 | 752 | 392 | 296 | 280 | 146 |
| Plants | Birds | Mammals | Mollusks | Fishes | insects | Reptiles | Crustaceans | Amphibians |
| 11% | 12% | 25% | 1% | 3% | 0.05% | 3% | 1% | 3% |
| Percentage under threat | | | | | | | | |

sedentary lifestyle, this surplus food is leading to national populations that are overweight, and with a significant part of their population clinically obese. This leads to an increase in health problems, such as heart disease. This contrasts with science fiction stories in which the only growth area of the human body is the brain.

Will the human brain grow larger still, or has its evolution peaked? We do not know. There is no direction to evolution, in the sense that it is moving toward something. It just works on the variation that appears in a population.

Will the population continue to grow? Maybe, but there is hope that populations will eventually stabilize, or even reduce in future centuries. In developed countries there is already little growth. Perhaps when disease kills fewer in infancy, the need for a large family lessens, so people prefer to have fewer children and a more comfortable lifestyle instead. Where developing nations become more prosperous, they too begin to experience a dip in birthrate. This can only happen worldwide if resources are distributed fairly enough for everyone to be prosperous.

**DID YOU KNOW?**
Genetic "faults" such as poor eyesight or weak physique are no longer removed from the human population in a way they might have been thousands, or even hundreds of years ago. Survivors breed to pass on these faults. But in the last few years, we have learned much about the genetic basis of some diseases. As time goes on it may be possible to "correct" many of the genetic faults of individuals.

*What does the future hold?*
*Having exhausted the natural resources of the Earth, the human race may eventually cause its own extinction.*

| Million years ago | Events |
|---|---|
| 5,000–4,000 | 4,550 Formation of the Earth |
| 4,000–2,000 | 3,600 Origins of life |
| | 2,400 First organisms with a cell nucleus |
| 2,000–400 | 1,400 First multicellular organisms |
| | 455 First land plants |
| | 445 Ice age |
| | 417 First land animals |
| 400–6 | 325 First reptiles |
| | 300 Ice age |
| | 230 First dinosaurs |
| | 210 First mammals |
| | 65 Extinction of dinosaurs |
| | 55 Early primates |
| | 14 First *Ramapithecus* |
| | 10 First *Gigantopithecus* |
| *Gigantopithecus* | 8 Last common ancestor of humans and apes |
| 6–2 | 6.0 "Millennium man"—*Orrorin tugensis* and *Sahelanthropus tchadensis* in existence |
| | 5.8 *Ardipithecus ramidus* in existence |
| | 4.0 First Australopithecines; *Australopithecus afarensis* |
| | 3.0 *Australopithecus africanus* in existence |
| *Australopithecines* | 2.5 *Australopithecus boisei* in existence |
| 2–0.0035 | 2.0 First *Australopithecus robustus* |
| | 1.9 First *Homo erectus* |
| | 1.7 Ice age |
| | 0.25 Emergence of Neanderthals |
| | 0.19 Emergence of *Homo sapiens* in Africa |
| | 0.04 Fully modern Cro-Magnon man in Europe |
| | 0.035 Disappearance of Neanderthals |
| | 0.005 Bronze Age begins |
| *Cro-Magnon man* | 0.0035 Iron Age begins |

Fossils help scientists determine when different kinds of plants and animals first appeared.

| Era | Millions of years ago | Period | Main events | |
| --- | --- | --- | --- | --- |
| Proterozoic Eon | 2,500–543 | Proterozoic periods | | bacteria, simple animals, and plants exist |
| Paleozoic | 543–490 | Cambrian | | sea animals without a backbone flourish |
| | 490–443 | Ordovician | | early fish appear |
| | 443–417 | Silurian | | land plants and land arthropods appear |
| | 417–354 | Devonian | | insects and amphibians appear |
| | 354–290 | Carboniferous | | reptiles and flying insects live in forests |
| | 290–248 | Permian | | reptiles dominate |
| Mesozoic | 248–206 | Triassic | | dinosaurs dominate, mammals appear |
| | 206–144 | Jurassic | | birds appear and pterosaurs flourish |
| | 144–65 | Cretaceous | | flowering plants appear |
| Cenozoic | 65–1.8 | Tertiary | | dinosaurs die out, mammals spread |
| | 1.8–present | Quaternary | | humans dominate |

*Acheulean hand axe*

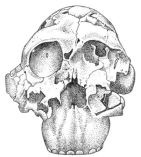

*Australopithecine*

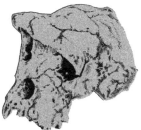

*Brow ridge*

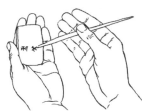

*Cuneiform writing*

**aboriginal**  Describes people inhabiting a land from early times before the arrival of colonists.

**Acheulean** (or **Acheulian**) Describes the culture and artifacts of a period of the Stone Age. Named after a village called St Acheul in northern France, where such artifacts were first found.

**archaic**  Old-fashioned; of a very early period.

**arthritis**  A disease in which joints become inflamed and painful.

**artifact**  An object that has been made by humans, rather than by natural forces.

**aurochs**  The wild ox, a type of wild cattle that lived in Europe in prehistoric times.

**australopithecine**  A member of the group of primates that lived from about four million to one million years ago and had a mixture of apelike and humanlike characteristics.

**basalt**  A fine-grained dark rock of volcanic origin.

**Broca's area**  A lobe on the lower left of the brain that is thought to have responsibility for speech.

**brow ridge**  A pronounced ridge on the skull above the eyes that is prominent in some apes and early men.

**calorie**  A unit in which heat is measured. It is also used for measuring the amount of energy in food.

**carrion**  The flesh of dead animals, found rather than killed by the animal eating it.

**chert**  A rock made of silica, similar to flint.

**Cro-Magnon**  A name given to early modern humans in Europe, named after the place in southwest France where their remains were found.

**cuneiform**  Describes a type of writing using wedge-shaped (cunei-form) marks in clay, as used in ancient Babylon.

**demotic**  Of the people; a simplified form of ancient Egyptian writing.

**DNA** (**deoxyribonucleic acid**), the chemical that carries the code for constructing the cells and body of most living things. It is passed on from parents to offspring.

**domestication**  The process of taming animals for use as farm animals, beasts of burden, or companions.

**extinct**  Describes a type of animal or plant no longer living.

**femur**  The thigh bone, the top bone of the leg.

**fluoride**  A compound containing the element fluorine that is present in many soils into which water containing it has seeped.

**fossil**  The remains, found in rocks, of an animal or plant that was once alive.

**frontal** At the front; the frontal bone of the skull at the forehead; or the frontal lobe of the brain, important in memory.

**furnace** Enclosed oven for the intense heating of metals.

**genus** A group of very closely-related species.

**glaciation** In a state of being covered by ice sheets or glaciers.

**glacier** A mass of ice formed on land, usually from accumulated snowfall.

**global warming** A term applied to the perceived increase in global temperature due to humans burning fossil fuels, etc.

**groundwater** Water found in crevices in rocks and soil.

*Frontal lobe*

**hieratic** Of priests: describes a simplified form of hieroglyphic writing used in ancient Egypt by priests.

**hieroglyphics** Writing in which a picture represents a word or sound.

**hominid** A member of the family that includes modern humans and their ancient ancestors.

**hybrid** The offspring of parents of two different varieties or species.

**ice age** A cool period in the Earth's history when sheets of ice spread across considerable areas of the continents.

**interglacial** A period of milder climate between periods of heavy glaciation.

**larynx** The voice box.

**Levallois** A type of stone toolmaking in which flakes were struck from a core; named after a Parisian suburb where substantial evidence of the technique was found.

**linguistic** Relating to language.

**mammal** Warm-blooded animal that feeds its young on milk. Mammals usually have hair.

**mammary** The milk-secreting glands of mammals, or human breasts.

**matrix** The lump of rock in which a fossil is embedded.

**melanin** A black pigment which colors the skin and hair in humans and other animals.

**Mesoamerica** Southern Mexico, Guatemala, and Honduras.

**mitochondrion** An organelle, or distinct region, of a cell in which respiration and energy production takes place.

**mutation** A change in genetic material.

**Neanderthal** A type of human, named after the Neander Valley where they were first found.

**occipital** The region at the back of the skull.

**omnivore** Describes an animal that eats both plants and meat.

**opposable** Capable of being placed opposite, like the human thumb to the rest of the fingers.

**paleoanthropologist** A person who studies people of the past.

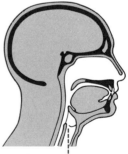

*Furnace*

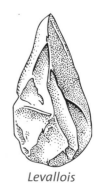

*Larynx*

*Levallois*

© DIAGRAM

*Neanderthal*

**papyrus** A type of reed that grows in swamps in Africa, from stems of which a type of paper used by the ancient Egyptians was made.

**parietal** A bone running from the side to the top of the skull.

**pharaoh** A king of ancient Egypt.

**pictogram** As pictograph.

**pictograph** A picture representing a word, syllable, or phrase.

**Pleistocene** A geological epoch covering most of the last two million years, notable for encompassing the great Ice Age.

**predator** An animal that catches and kills other animals for food.

**quartzite** A rock containing quartz, derived from sandstone that has been subjected to volcanic heat.

**quench** To cool by plunging into water.

**rickets** A childhood disease caused by a lack of Vitamin D. Victims are unable to take in, and use, calcium, and the bones are softened and deformed.

**savanna** A tropical grassland.

**scavenge** To search for items of food, such as carrion.

**sickle** A tool with a sharp blade and a handle used for cutting stalks of grain.

**species** In biology, a group of individuals that can potentially breed with each other. What in everyday speech is meant by a kind of animal, for example, lion or tiger. Each species has its own two-part scientific name. Our own species is *Homo sapiens*.

**syllable** A segment of a word that makes a single sound.

**tundra** A treeless, cold area with low vegetation in polar regions or mountain tops.

**ultraviolet** Short wavelength light just beyond the range that is visible to our eyes. It can have damaging effects on some types of skin.

**Vitamin D** One of the group of vitamins essential in small amounts to the body for its proper functioning.

**Wernicke's area** A small area at the side of the brain important for understanding speech and organizing its content.

**yeti** A manlike animal, probably mythical, reputed to live high in the Himalayas.

*Pictograph*

*Sickle*

# Websites to visit

There is a lot of useful information on the internet. There are also many sites that are fun to use. Remember that you may be able to get information on a particular topic by using a search engine such as Google (*http://www.google.com*). Some of the sites that are found in this way may be very useful, others not. Below is a selection of websites related to the material covered by this book. Most are illustrated, and they are mainly of the type that provides useful facts.

Facts On File, Inc. *takes no responsibility for the information contained within these websites. All the sites were accessible as of September 1, 2003.*

**A Look At Modern Human Origins**
Scholarly research in paleoanthropology.
*http://www.modernhumanorigins.com*

**Anthropology Resources**
Lists internet resources for the study of man.
*http://www.qozi.com/anthropology/*

**Archaeology Info**
Archeological site with an emphasis on human evolution.
*http://www.archaeologyinfo.com*

**Arizona State University, Institute of Human Origins**
An academic site dedicated to the recovery and analysis of the fossil evidence for human evolution.
*http://www.asu.edu/clas/iho/*

**BBC Walking with Beasts: *Australopithecus***
An animated account of australopithecines.
*http://www.bbc.co.uk/beasts/evidence/prog4/page2.shtml*

**BBC Walking with Cavemen**
An interactive educational site depicting human evolution through reconstructions.
*http://www.bbc.co.uk/science/cavemen/*

**California State University, Department of Anthropology: Ancestors**
Photographs of hominid skulls.
*http://www.csus.edu/anth/physanth/ancestor.htm*

**Dover Museum: The Bronze Age Boat**
The world's oldest seagoing boat, with links to European Bronze Age information.
*http://www.dover.gov.uk/museum/boat/*

**Minnesota State University, E-Museum: Human Evolution**
A brief guide to hominids.
*http://www.mnsu.edu/emuseum/biology/humanevolution/*

*National Geographic* On-line
The website of the acclaimed magazine includes many relevant news articles.
*http://www.nationalgeographic.com*

*Nature*
Science news from the online journal.
*http://www.nature.com*

**Neanderthals and Modern Humans–A Regional Guide**
Information on Neanderthals and modern humans, with links to many archaeological sites.
*http://www.neanderthal-modern.com*

*New Scientist*
Online news from the world of science.
*http://www.newscientist.com*

**Open Directory Project: Human Evolution**
A comprehensive listing of internet resources.
*http://dmoz.org/Science/Biology/Evolution/Human/*

*Scientific American*
News from the world of science and technology.
*http://www.sciam.com*

**Smithsonian Institution: Human Origins Program**
A guide to current research, with excellent photographs and illustrations.
*http://www.mnh.si.edu/anthro/humanorigins/*

**The Talk Origins Archive: Hominid Species**
Lists hominid species as a reference for newsgroup discussions.
*http://www.talkorigins.org/faqs/homs/species.html*

**UNESCO: Peking Man World Heritage Site at Zhoukoudian**
Describes the discoveries at Zhoukoudian.
*http://www.unesco.org/ext/field/beijing/whc/pkm-site.htm*

# Index